A HISTORY
OF MODERN CHINA

BY

KENNETH SCOTT LATOURETTE

Sterling Professor of Missions and Oriental History, Emeritus,
and Associate Fellow of Berkeley College
in Yale University

*

PENGUIN BOOKS

MELBOURNE · LONDON · BALTIMORE

Penguin Books Ltd, Harmondsworth, Middlesex

U.S.A. : Penguin Books Inc., 3300 Clipper Mill Road, Baltimore 11, Md
(*Educational Representative:*
D. C. Heath & Co., 285 Columbus Avenue, Boston 16, Mass)

CANADA : Penguin Books (Canada) Ltd, 47 Green Street,
Saint Lambert, Montreal, P.Q.

AUSTRALIA : Penguin Books Pty Ltd, 762 Whitehorse Road,
Mitcham, Victoria

SOUTH AFRICA : Penguin Books (S.A.) Pty Ltd, Gibraltar House,
Regents Road, Sea Point, Cape Town

—

First published 1954

Made and printed in Great Britain
by The Whitefriars Press Ltd,
London and Tonbridge

CONTENTS

EDITORIAL FOREWORD

THE present mental, social, and political habit of every country in the world is the product of that country's record and tradition. *A History of Modern China*, like all the books planned in this series of Pelicans devoted to world history, is designed to give to readers intelligent and scholarly assistance in answering the questions 'Why is China what it is, and how has it become what it is?' The more distant past, therefore, is given in less detail than that history which can be directly connected with events as we see them to-day.

It is often urged that world history is best written without the limitations of frontiers, that, for example, a history of the development of Western Europe has more historical validity than 'nationalist' histories of France, Germany, the Low Countries, and Britain. Nevertheless it is national character, national development, and national power, which incite the curiosity of most of us, and it is these things which seem to be behind most of the international problems with which we are faced to-day. Therefore, in preparing the plan of THE PELICAN HISTORY OF THE WORLD it has been decided that the old and familiar emphasis upon national history has meant sufficient to justify its continuance in this series.

Each volume is written by a specialist, and the emphasis given to such matters as trade, religion, politics, foreign relations, intellectual and social life, varies and must vary between volume and volume, but the interplay of nationalisms is as much part of national history as internal events, and it is hoped that THE PELICAN HISTORY OF THE WORLD will be both a series of national histories and, in the true sense, a history of the modern world.

Among the early books in the series, in addition to the present one, will be:

History of Modern France by J. A. Cobban, Professor of French History, University College, London

History of Spain and Portugal by W. C. Atkinson, Stevenson Professor of Spanish, Glasgow University

History of the United States; Vol. 1: *Colonies to Nation*; Vol. 2: *Nation to World Power* by J. E. Morpurgo and Russel B. Nye, Professor at Michigan State College

J. E. MORPURGO

PREFACE

THE year was 1910. The scene was a provincial capital in the heart of China. The city was over 2,000 years old and was proud of its history and its conservatism. Around it was an ancient wall mounted with obsolete cannon. It was criss-crossed with narrow streets which in the day-time were thronged, were redolent with the odours of opium, night soil, and the frying foods of street vendors, streets which resounded with the cries of the hawkers of various wares and the bearers of sedan chairs, the squeak of ungreased wheelbarrows, the squeal of pigs being carried to market, and the pleas of beggars. As one passed along the streets he could look in upon numerous handicrafts – the making of shoes, the dyeing of cloth, the manufacture of paper money for burning on behalf of the dead, and huge pestles operated by human feet for the hulling of rice. Hidden behind blank walls were the courtyards of the mansions of the rich, some of them with treasures of books and of paintings of old masters. Narrow side alleys led to the crowded tenements of the poor. Trade, handicrafts, and even beggars and thieves were organized by guilds. In the city was the yamen of the provincial governor, representative of the imperial power of distant Peking and of the Confucian state, a set of political institutions under which, with modifications, the Chinese had lived for over two millenniums. There were Confucian temples, symbolic of the moral and intellectual ideas which had been dominant for twenty centuries and the scene of ceremonial gatherings of the scholar-officials who, nurtured in Confucianism and its exponents and guard-ians, were the *élite* who by precept and example set the standards of conduct of the country. Near the heart of the city was an open space which until a few years before had been occupied by rows of small covered stalls in which were given periodically the highly competitive examinations based upon the Confucian classics through which entrance was had to the coveted ranks of the scholar class and the

7

civil service. At nightfall the gates in the encompassing battlements were closed and the streets were empty. The city then seemed like a vast house, with 200,000 or more inhabitants enclosed within a wall which was about a mile wide and a mile and a half long, in rooms of various sizes separated by narrow halls which echoed to the gong and bamboo drum of the night-watchman as he made his rounds.

Outside the city were countless graves, some of them dating from before the Christian era. Across the river, on the slopes and at the summit of a mountain were a Buddhist and a Taoist monastery, representative of religions which had long been present in China, the one an importation and a channel of Indian influence, and the other native to China.

Life went on much as it had for untold generations. Here was a great civilization with a long history, the creation and the possession of a proud people who traditionally had regarded all foreigners as crude barbarians. Here was a world seemingly as apart from the rest of mankind as though it were on a distinct planet.

Yet in that year there were evidences of an invasion from another world. On an island in the river were the houses of consuls of Western Powers, the homes of merchants, and the dwellings of British subjects who were managing the customs service, a system imposed on China from the outside half a century and more earlier. On the river bank were the offices of European and American business firms. British and Japanese steamers connected the city with down-river marts through which flowed the products of the factories of the industrialized Occident and of Japan. Lamps fed by the kerosene refined and imported by foreigners were supplanting older forms of lighting. From time to time foreign gunboats lay in the river as a protection for the invaders. Within the walls were homes, churches, schools, and an incipient hospital and medical and nursing school of Christian missionaries from Europe and America, vivid evidence that this other world was already effecting an entrance. To the east and south were the beginnings of cuts and embankments which were designed to carry a railway which would form the path for the iron horse, 'the fire-wheel wagon', to form a road for additional penetration. The vacant plot where once had been the examination stalls was mute evidence that the old order had been dealt a mortal blow at its very heart.

Here was an early stage of a vast revolution, a revolution as great as though men from Mars had forced themselves and their civilization upon the inhabitants of the earth.

By the 1950's the revolution had proceeded much further. The crenellated wall had long since disappeared. The railroad had been completed, a trunk line between the north and south, with gateways to the invaders at both ends. New streets had been driven through the city. Electric light, the telephone, and the automobile had appeared. The Confucian monarchy had been abandoned and with its going the local representatives of the central government had shifted again and again. In place of the monarchy there had come what was called a republic, but the Chinese had floundered in their attempts to adopt and adapt institutions and ideals with which they were unfamiliar. Civil war had racked the country. In a prolonged Japanese invasion the battle lines had more than once moved back and forth across the city, leaving much of it a smoking ruin. Rebuilding was rapid, but had not been accomplished when a new and even more revolutionary invasion, that of Communism of the Russian pattern, took possession. In all of these changes the schools shared and through them successive student generations were moulded. Confucianism as the standard of education was swept into the dustbin and its passing created a void which for a growing minority was filled by Christianity, but which left the majority empty and dissatisfied, potential converts to the dogmatic ideology of Communism. Social customs, including the relations between the sexes and marriage, were kaleidoscopic. The river still ran and opposite loomed the familiar hills, but had those returned who had known the city only in 1910 they would have been left breathless and bewildered by the changes.

The scene has been paralleled by similar ones in other parts of the world. Beginning tentatively in the thirteenth century, resumed late in the fifteenth century but pressed most vigorously in the nineteenth and twentieth centuries, there had been a global movement by which the peoples of Western Europe had made their way into all the inhabited parts of the globe. In great areas, notably the Americas, Australia, and New Zealand, by the mid twentieth century these peoples were dominant in numbers as well as in culture. In Africa, in the islands of the Pacific, and in the densely peopled portions of South and East Asia and the fringing islands until recently in most areas they had been dominant politically, ruling groups whose commerce, capital, and manners were permeating all phases of the collective life. In the mid-century, although their political control was disappearing, many aspects of their civilization continued to be copied. In the rest of the world, notably Eastern Europe including especially Russia and the northern reaches of Asia which were part of the Russian Empire, ideas and the mechanical appliances of life were more and more from Western Europe.

Everywhere they went, Western European peoples and their civilization made for changes, many of them profound. Those changes mounted as the twentieth century progressed. That was partly because Western Europe itself was in the grip of a swelling revolution, a revolution which was seen in every aspect of life. Led by Western European peoples and stimulated by ideas, techniques, learning, religion, and institutions which came from them, all mankind was on the march, leaving behind much of the old and familiar and entering a new age whose main outlines could as yet be only partly discerned.

Among no other people was the revolution on as gargantuan a scale as among the Chinese. That was partly because the Chinese were the largest fairly homogeneous group of mankind. At the dawn of the twentieth century they were usually said to number 400 millions. All Western Europe, although much more varied, did not have as many. Nor did all the Americas. The vast Russian Empire could not claim half that total. Even India fell short of it by nearly a fourth and, moreover, did not present nearly so uniform a cultural, ethnic, and linguistic front to the invading culture. In China the revolution was particularly impressive because of the richness and the maturity of the culture which was being displaced. So-called 'primitive' cultures usually succumb more quickly to the impact of an 'advanced' culture, such as that of Western Europe, than does one 'advanced' culture before another ' advanced' culture. Across the centuries the Chinese had produced a civilization which, far from being 'primitive', in such achievements as art, literature, philosophy, and political and social institutions, could stand comparison with what had thus far been accomplished by any other people. Yet now, in the twentieth century, that civilization was being more drastically altered than any other which could be said to be 'advanced'. By the middle of that century the changes were more sweeping than those in any other centre of high culture. They were greater than those among Western European peoples, whether in Europe itself, in the Americas, in Australasia, or South Africa. They were much more drastic than those in India, the Near East, and Japan. Even those in Russia, spectacular though they were, had not been as basically revolutionary. Only what was taking place in that greatest aggregation of 'primitive' peoples, the Africans south of the Sahara, was carrying away as much of the past in a vast segment of mankind.

Significantly and soberingly, in the mid twentieth century the revolution in China appeared to be far from having reached its end. Later generations might see that it was then only in its early stages. We say 'significantly and soberingly ' because of what the revolution was already meaning not only for the hundreds of millions of Chinese, but also for the Far East in general and for all the rest of mankind. The second World War of the century had really had its first stages in China, in the invasions by the Japanese in 1931 and 1937. These invasions had dealt a fatal blow to the League of Nations, the organization through which the world had been attempting to achieve global order and peace. In the 1950's the participation of the Chinese Communists in a war in Korea was a major factor in a crucial testing of the successor of the League of Nations, the United Nations. The world could not ignore the changes in China. If it sought to do so, they would inescapably claim its attention. Particularly did they concern that world, the world of the Occident, which had forced itself upon China and from which the revolutionary forces were sprung.

This volume is called *A History of Modern China*. It is the story of these changes in China which is its primary theme. Yet the changes cannot be understood or appreciated unless they are set against the background of the entire course of China's pilgrimage. In an attempt to appreciate the effects of the natural environment on that history, we begin, as is fitting, with a brief account of the geographic setting. Next follows a section, about a sixth of the book, on the history and culture of China before the time when, in the third quarter of the nineteenth century, the impact of the West began to bring the first stages of the revolution. Here only the main outlines are given, and they primarily in such fashion as will help to make intelligible the developments of the nineteenth and twentieth centuries. The major portion of the book is devoted to the hundred years or so which lie between the 1850s and the mid-1950s. It seeks to summarize these decades. It endeavours to reflect something of their thrilling and absorbing interest, to point out their meaning for China, and to hint at their bearing upon that western world from which came the impulses which broke up the old and entered into the new. For the most part details will be avoided and only the men, events, and movements will be singled out which appear to be of major importance for an understanding of the era. Finally, a brief bibliography will be appended, made up of a rigorously selected list designed as an indication of works in which more detailed information can be obtained by those who desire it.

No historian can write without a bias. If he professes to do so he is either blind to it and deceiving himself or is seeking to put his readers off their guard. So far as the present author is aware of his bias it may be described in about the following terms. He is a historian by training and long practice as a teacher and author. He is from the Occident, and so inevitably views the revolution from outside China and not as would a Chinese. He was in China as a teacher in a Christian school and witnessed some of the early stages of the revolution as he saw them in the city described in the opening paragraphs. In the intervening years he has watched with absorbed interest the course of the revolution. He has known many of the participants, both Chinese and foreign. He is an American and intensely critical of the Communism which has marked what in the 1950's is the latest stage of the revolution. Yet he holds no brief for the policies and actions of the United States and he seeks to divest himself of a distinctively American perspective. Nor would he make of these chapters an anti-Communist tract. He endeavours to view the scene as objectively as possible. He is fully aware that many interpretations of this story have been given and will be given. He can simply hope that the following pages will aid in some degree to clarify a series of events and movements which are of major importance for all mankind.

CHINA

CHAPTER ONE

THE GEOGRAPHIC SETTING

GREAT though the changes were in the China of the nine-teenth and especially of the twentieth century, the geo-graphic and climatic factors remained fairly constant. From the dawn of history they had helped to shape the people, their institutions and culture. They continued to do so.

China as seen on the maps of the nineteenth and twentieth centuries consists of two main divisions, what are sometimes called China proper and the outlying dependencies.

China proper is the region in which live the vast majority of the Chinese. It comprises about 1,500,000 square miles and has therefore about two-fifths the area of Europe and about seventeen times that of Great Britain. Much of it is in the valleys of the two great systems of the Huang (Yellow) and Yangtze Rivers. These streams have their rise in the great mass of plateaus and mountains in Central Asia where are also born the major rivers of India, Burma, Thailand, and Indochina. The Huang (or Yellow) River takes its name from the sediment with which it is heavily laden and which is chiefly from the loess, a fine, friable, fertile soil which blan-kets much of the northern part of China proper. Originally largely wind-blown, much of the loess has been re-sorted by streams. Easily eroded, it burdens the Yellow River. From this sediment the latter, confined by dykes, some natural and some artificial, has built up a bed which in some stretches is higher than the surrounding plain. From time to time it has broken through its restraining embankments in disastrous floods, and more than once it has cut a new course to the sea, now north and now south of the mountainous Shantung promontory. It has thus earned the name 'China's sorrow'. The Yangtze, a larger stream, is navigable through most of its course. On its lower reaches it is plied by ocean-going craft. Like the Yellow River it is subject to floods. With the Yellow River and some smaller streams it has built up an alluvial plain in the east of China proper, most of it fertile, which has been made to support some of the densest rural populations on the globe. In the upper part of the valley of the Yangtze and its tributaries, and separated from the lower portion by ranges of mountains through which the river cuts its way in deep gorges, is a region, much of which has been comprised in the province of Szechwan and at the heart of which there is an extraordinarily fertile and well watered area, the Red Basin, which also maintains a large population.

Not all China proper is in the valleys of the Yellow and Yangtze Rivers and their tributaries. Between the two valleys there is a mountain system, a kind of tongue stretching out from the main mass in the heart of the continent. South of the mouth of the Yangtze the coast is bounded by mountains and is indented, in some places deeply, by estuaries which provide inviting harbours. In the far south is the Hsi Kiang, or West River, not as large as the Huang or the Yangtze, but having a delta near the upper end of which has long been one of the major ports of China proper, Canton. The south-west is a mountainous tableland, an extended and lower spur from the great mountain mass to the west.

China proper is fitted by nature to be the home of a highly civilized and populous nation. While within it there are distinct regions, the barriers are not so great as to prevent political and cultural unity. For more than half the time since the third century before Christ most of it has been under one central government. While geography is not entirely nor perhaps chiefly determinative, it has made important contributions. The region has an abundance of fertile soil. Some of this is in the numerous river valleys and alluvial plains. Much is in the loess uplands of the north. The mountains have supplied the timber that has been used extensively in buildings, in ships, and in the charcoal which has been one of the fuels of the land. Mineral resources in iron and the other metals were ample for a pre-industrial culture. In several minerals, notably coal, China proper is well equipped for the industrial age. However, it lacks some

of the minerals in sufficient supply for the highly industrialized twentieth century. It is weak in iron and is notably deficient in petroleum. The climate is favourable. Most of the
land is in the temperate zone. The rains are monsoonal. In
the spring the air over the great interior of Asia in the north
and west heats more rapidly than the oceans on the south
and west. Partly as a consequence, moisture-laden winds
from the south move northward, dropping their water as
they go. As a result, rainfall is heavy on the south coast and
is much less in the north. On the northern border of China
proper it becomes so slight that only in good years is it adequate for cultivated crops, and flocks and herds subsisting
on grazing become a major source of livelihood. Most of the
rain is in the growing season. In the autumn, the interior
land masses cool more quickly than the oceans and the prevailing winds are from the north and are dry. In the south
and the Yangtze Valley the major grain is rice. In the north
wheat, millet, and kaoliang (a kind of sorghum with grain
about the size of a small pea) are dominant.

During the nineteenth and the fore part of the twentieth
century the outlying dependencies which were considered a
part of the Chinese Empire were Manchuria, Mongolia,
Sinkiang (or Chinese Turkestan), and Tibet. Through them
China had the widest extent in its history. Additional border
areas had a looser connexion as tribute-bearing states in a
relation different from any of the patterns familiar to the
Occident. They were chiefly Korea, Annam, and Burma.

Manchuria is so called because it was the home of the
Manchus, who conquered China in the seventeenth century
and governed it until 1912. More than once under China's
greatest dynasties the southern part had been ruled from
China proper. However, until the twentieth century the
Chinese population was sparse. In the twentieth century
Manchuria rapidly filled with Chinese until they formed the
overwhelming majority of the population. It was then more
and more regarded by the Chinese as an integral part of
their country and was latterly denominated by them not
Manchuria, as though it were a semi-alien bordering de-

pendency, but the north-eastern provinces, by right included in China proper. Rich in fertile soil, forests, and minerals, among the latter both coal and iron, its potential in wealth in the industrialized twentieth century was enormous. Desired by the three great peoples who bordered on it, the Chinese, the Russians, and the Japanese, it became a bone of contention among them. It will therefore enter prominently into our story.

Mongolia, drawing its name from the Mongols, is a vast region west of Manchuria and north of China proper. The portion known as Inner Mongolia borders on the latter and the line between the two is not clearly defined. An area of marginal rainfall, some of it has been brought under cultivation, especially in periods when the precipitation has been greater than at others. Much of it is grazing land. What in the nineteenth century constituted the majority of the population, the Mongols, drew their subsistence from flocks and herds and were semi-nomadic, organized by tribes. As the population in China mounted, especially in the twentieth century, more and more Chinese pressed into Inner Mongolia. Farmers, they put it into tillage and planted crops, thus encroaching on traditional Mongol territory. North of Inner Mongolia stretched the Gobi, a great desert. North of the Gobi lies Outer Mongolia, largely mountains and steppe. Its wealth has consisted chiefly in its herds. This is the historic seat of the Mongols. From it in the thirteenth century, led by Jenghiz Khan, they burst to conquer China, Korea, much of Central and Western Asia, and the southern part of what is now Russia. Although brought within the empire of the Manchus late in the seventeenth century, to the Chinese it was alien territory and the few who went there were chiefly officials and merchants. It was not strange that with the disorders in China proper attendant upon the decline of the Manchus and the stormy years of the republic, it broke away, became independent, and was eventually drawn within the Russian orbit.

Sinkiang, 'the New Dominion', was given its name because it was brought into the empire of the Manchus shortly after the middle of the eighteenth century, later than Mongolia and Tibet. Yet this was not the first time that it had been conquered by the rulers of China. A corridor, much of it low-lying, between the north-west of China proper and Central and Western Asia, through it were the caravan routes by which much of the foreign trade entered China before the nineteenth century saw the coming of the West in force by way of the sea. From it also issued some of the invaders of China proper. The strongest Chinese dynasties, therefore, brought it under their control. Much of it is desert. Its southern and larger portion is mostly contained in the basin of the Tarim River, a stream which flows eastward and empties into a marshy salt lake, the Lob Nor. To the north of the Tarim Valley is the lofty T'ien Shan, from the slopes of which drain streams on whose courses are some of the oases which support the population and help to make the east-west roads possible. Because it is a corridor, Sinkiang is an ethnic mixture, with a population containing deposits left by many invaders and travellers. In it the Chinese have been and are a minority, although from time to time a ruling and therefore an important minority.

Tibet is a huge and lofty tableland, fringed by mountain systems which include the highest peaks on the planet. Three-fourths of the plateau which constitutes the bulk of Tibet is over 10,000 ft. high. To the south are the Himalayas and the breath-taking canyons which are the upper courses of the Brahmaputra, the Indus, and the Sutlej. To the west are the Pamirs and the Karakoram Mountains. On the north are other mountains, some of which tower 20,000 or more feet above the level of the sea. To the east, as a barrier between Tibet and China proper, are ranges, one peak of which is more than 25,000 ft. high. Most of the scanty population is in valleys in the eastern portions of the plateau. Much of the subsistence is from herds.

The outlying dependencies have played an important role in the history of China. So extensive and formidable are they that in the days before steam made the seas a highway, they tended to shut China off from other civilized peoples. As we shall see, many influences penetrated China from other cultures, both by sea and by land. Yet in the main the Chinese were self-sufficient and their culture was chiefly their own creation. Knowing intimately only peoples of cultures which they deemed inferior and barbarous, they thought of their civilization as of right universal and embracing all mankind. This isolation may in part account for the thoroughgoing character of the revolution which we are to describe. As we have suggested, the inherited culture of China has been more nearly swept away by the impact of the Occident and of the forces of the twentieth century than has any other which may be called advanced. This may be to some degree due to the fact that, while many times conquered in whole or in part by invaders, the latter either adopted Chinese culture or were eventually driven out, but, in contrast, in the twentieth century the Chinese deliberately adopted what came to them from the West, whether that was directly from the Occident or indirectly through Japan and latterly through Russia.

It must be noted, moreover, that until the nineteenth century the chief threats to China's independence were from these border lands rather than from the sea. From them were the peoples who from time to time made themselves masters of portions of China proper. Twice, indeed, came those who conquered all of it, first the Mongols and then the Manchus. It is not strange, therefore, that as they strove for security the Chinese faced landward rather than seaward. The westward and northward orientation was symbolized by the Great Wall. First erected before the Christian era and repaired and enlarged many times later, it stretched along all the northern border of China proper. It has been said, although that is debatable, that it is the only work of men's hands before the construction of railways which could be seen from the Moon.

This landward mentality may be responsible for the

failure of the Chinese to become a maritime power. Only once, and that briefly in the early fifteenth century, did the Chinese launch formidable naval expeditions. When, in the nineteenth and twentieth centuries, invaders came from the sea, first from the Occident and then from Japan, China was quite unprepared by tradition effectively to resist them. In the nineteenth and twentieth centuries the threat from the land did not disappear. It was then from Russia. In the nineteenth century China lost more territory to Russia than to any other foreign Power. In the twentieth century there came the conquest of China by an ideology which entered from Russia and which tied China closely to that land. This proved a greater threat to their cultural integrity and independence than any other which the Chinese had known.

CHAPTER TWO

THE COURSE OF PRE-REVOLUTIONARY CHINESE HISTORY

WITH this geographic background as a setting, we can attempt to sketch the rise and development of what we may call the old China. This was the China which in the twentieth century underwent the gigantic revolution brought by the impact of the West and of the ideas and mechanical appliances which had their origin in the West. Here we must content ourselves merely with broad outlines, seeking to discern the main forces which shaped the China which in the nineteenth century began to succumb to the West and the major movements which were seen along the way.

Our knowledge of man in China takes us back into a remote antiquity. In the twentieth century there came to light in a cave in the north bones of what because of their location is known as Peking man, or, more technically, as Sinanthropus. Here was a primitive man who lived scores of thousands of years ago. A feature of his skull may indicate that the modern Chinese have him among their ancestors. Later, but still very remote, is evidence of old Stone Age man underneath the mantle of loess and thus ante-dating its deposit. Still later are remains, more abundant and varied, of new Stone Age man. Much of these is in the form of pottery. Some is in stone implements and some in the traces of dwellings, partly below the level of the surrounding earth. They show that there was not one civilization, but several cultures, possible indications of diverse races and origins. Where these peoples came from and who they were we do not know. We wait for archeology to tell us more. It seems significant that much of the evidence is in the north. It may point to migrations of people or cultural forms from Central and Western Asia along the corridor which leads into the north-west of China proper. Yet some and perhaps much may have come from the south. Between these new Stone Age cultures and the China of subsequent centuries no sharp break occurred. There was a continuous development.

Chinese legends and myths which became part of the familiar folk-lore profess to tell of beginnings and give accounts of ancient rulers. Among the latter were the 'model emperors' Yao, Shun, and Yü, who were held to be paragons of virtue, giving themselves wholly to the welfare of their subjects. The third of them, Yü, is said to have drained the land of a great flood and to have founded the first of the dynasties, Hsia. However, we cannot be certain that a reigning line of that name existed. If it did, its domains must have been small and were in the north, somewhere in the valley of the Yellow River.

Here is seen, presumably although not certainly read back by later generations, what became a pattern of Chinese history. That history moved by dynasties. Each of the major dynasties coincided with a distinct epoch in the life of China.

We are first on fairly firm ground in the first half of the second millennium before Christ. There was then in existence a state which we know as Shang. Chinese historians have called it the Shang (or Yin) Dynasty, the successor of the Hsia. Its centre was in the lower part of the valley of the Yellow River and it comprised much of the north-east of what we have described as China proper. In the present century the remains of its capital have been uncovered and we have learned much about it, supplementing what has been handed down in ancient Chinese writings. The Shang had a high and distinctive culture. So far as we know, it was purely a creation of the Chinese, with no influence from the outside. It had writing, through characters to which can be traced many of those now in use in China. It displayed great skill in the casting of bronze, beautiful examples of which have survived to this day. There were numerous domestic animals, among them the dog, the pig, fowls, and the elephant. Society was based upon agriculture. There seems to have been a marked class structure with a sharp division between the aristocracy and the common people. There were armies, and we hear of one which numbered at least 5,000. The chariot was in use. At the head of the state was a ruler with the title of Wang, and the position was kept in the same family. The Shang had a long duration, of about six centuries. The traditional dates are 1766–1122 B.C. While they are probably incorrect, the Shang period covered about the same number of years as that between Edward III of England and the middle of the twentieth century, and fully a third more than have elapsed since the discovery of America by Columbus.

The Shang were displaced and succeeded by the Chou. By their success the Chou inaugurated an era which bears their name and which continued for almost a millennium, until the middle of the third century before Christ. Here was a span of time much greater than that of the Shang, more than twice that of any later dynasty, and longer than that between the Norman conquest of England and our own day. It was marked by the gradual extension of what may be called Chinese culture over most of China proper north of and including the Yangtze Valley. The rule of the Chou was not effective over all this area. Indeed, the authority of the Wang, as the monarch was still called, declined and eventually was little more than ceremonial. The realm was more and more divided into a number of states, some large and some small. The period is often called feudal, but in the technical use of that term, as it was employed to describe what arose in Western Europe in the eighth, ninth, and tenth centuries and prevailed there in the Middle Ages and what was seen in Japan for several centuries, that designation is inaccurate. With local variations, the Chinese of the Chou were conscious of possessing a common culture and the conviction was cherished that all mankind should be one in civilization and under a unified administration headed by one ruler.

From these long centuries and this culture there came many contributions to the later China, some of which were still potent in the nineteenth century and early in the twentieth century. What became the classics, standard for literature, were chiefly from these times. They included what were later esteemed as the *Five Classics*, i.e. *The Classic of History* (*Shu Ching*), a collection of ancient documents, *The Classic of Poetry* (*Shih Ching*), an anthology of poems of many dates and authors, *The Spring and Autumn* (*Ch'un Ch'iu*), the annals of the state of Lu, long said to have been written or at least edited by Confucius, *The Record of Rites* (*Li Chi*), dealing with ritual and much of it from a later era, and *The Classic of Change* (*I Ching*), arising from practices of divination some of which went back to the Shang and possibly earlier. There were also many other books. Writing was largely on bamboo slips incised or written with a brush pen, and in characters which were a modified continuation of those of the Shang. The sharp distinction between social strata persisted from the Shang. The upper classes made much of the ceremonies in honour of their ancestors.

The Chou was especially marked by the development of schools of thought which were to contend for the mastery. All were to be remembered and to leave their impress on the later China. One of them, what is usually known in the West as Confucianism, although the term more often employed by the Chinese is *Ju Chiao*, or 'the Teaching of the Learned', was eventually to become dominant as the major body of ideas which shaped Chinese culture, but that was not until after the passing of the Chou.

The Chou, and especially the latter half of the Chou, was a time of intense intellectual ferment and vigorous debate. The focus of attention was largely on what constitutes ideal human conduct, and on the closely related subjects, the function and structure of society, including especially the family and the state. To anyone who thought more than superficially on these issues, it must have been clear that they could not be long discussed without entering into such questions as the nature of man and of the world in which man finds himself, and the relations of the two to each other. These, then, also became controversial topics. The approach, however, was primarily practical and utilitarian. Interest centred on the queries: What is the ideal society and how can that society be achieved? What in the broadest sense of that term is religion was inevitably involved and religious beliefs and ceremonies came in for discussion. Most of the scholars who engaged in the debates were socially and politically minded. Numbers of them either held political office or aspired so to do. Many of the discussions were at the courts of the princes of the states into which the realm was divided.

As its name indicates, Confucianism had as its most revered figure Confucius. Confucius, whose generally accepted dates are 551–479 B.C., did more to shape his people than any other individual in history. He early showed a deep interest in ceremonies and in the ways and records of the past and become their lifelong student. For a time he held office in his native state, but much of his later years he spent travelling from court to court, hoping vainly that he could find a ruler who would employ him on the high conditions which he laid down. A man of force of character and integrity, he was a teacher who attracted loyal disciples who recorded for posterity his words and his actions. A lover of music, conscientious, courteous, placing a high value upon the proprieties, dignified, but with a sense of humour, affable, serene, quietly assured that Providence had committed to him a mission, he carried through that assignment as a statesman and a teacher of ethics.

Deeply concerned for the disorder which he saw about him, Confucius held that it could be met by a return to what he believed to have been the policies of the model rulers of China's past. As a way of education and social control, he would have the ceremonies of antiquity revived and maintained, including those of religion. He held that if the upper classes, especially the monarchs, were upright and had the welfare of those below them at heart, the masses of men would be happy, contented, and peaceful. Government was to be more by moral influence than by force. He sought through his teaching and through companionship with his students to produce cultivated men of superior character. The example of men of this stamp would, he believed, lead others to imitate them, and thus the ideal society would be achieved.

Holding to much the same principles as Confucius, but more than a century after him, was Mencius, whose traditional dates are 373–288 B.C. Next to Confucius he was the teacher most honoured by the orthodox scholars of later generations. He, too, was interested in government and spent much of his life journeying from one capital to another of the states of his day, seeking to induce princes to accept his programme. Even more than Confucius, he insisted that if the rulers set worthy examples their subjects would conform to them. Consistently with this conviction, he held that men are by nature good and will respond if those who are over them are devoted to the welfare of those whom they govern.

In sharp contrast with Confucianism was a school which is generally called Taoism and which, next to Confucianism, was to be the most persistent. Its most highly esteemed expression is in the little book or tract, the *Tao Tê Ching*. Ascribed to Lao Tzŭ, whom the Taoists represented as being an older contemporary of Confucius, it is of much later date than the latter and of uncertain authorship. Of Lao Tzŭ almost nothing that is dependable is known, and it is sometimes said that he never existed. The *Tao Tê Ching* advocated, as the correct way for men and society, conformity to the *Tao*, a term long in use in Chinese thought, by which the Taoists meant the great reality which creates and controls the universe. Conformity with the *Tao* entailed what is sometimes called 'inaction', but which is probably better described as 'doing everything by doing nothing'. The *Tao Tê Ching* was critical of what was most prized by the Confucianists – the regard for elaborate ceremonies, the zealous cultivation of morals, and a highly organized government and economic structure. It advocated the simplest society possible. It decried the prizing of wealth, for were it not for that, so it said, there would be no coveting and no stealing. The *Tao Tê Ching* held up as the ideal a society in which village dwellers would be aware that there were other villages because they could hear their roosters crowing in the mornings, but would have no desire to know who dwelt in them. This meant no communication between villages, no commerce, and no elaborately ordered state.

In later centuries, as we are to see, Taoism was to undergo many changes. It was to take many forms. It was to become a religious cult, eventually borrowing from the imported Buddhism and having in it much of magic. It was to stress the achievement of personal immortality, a goal to be attained partly through diet and a physical and mental regimen, and entailing the search for the elixir of life. Yet through it many sensitive and thoughtful souls were seeking for a quietistic way of life, emancipated from the demands of a complex society.

Born in the small state of Lu in the present Shantung, as were Confucius and Mencius, younger than the former but older than the latter, was Mo Ti, also called Mo Tzŭ. For centuries his influence rivalled that of these two fellow products of that principality, but eventually it waned and he was remembered only by scholars and as one who had deviated from what later was regarded as orthodoxy. Deeply religious, he regarded the dominant power in the universe not as unvarying law, as was the tendency about him, but as a personal Supreme Being who, with the spirits, punishes those who do evil. He argued against the current scepticism regarding the existence of spirits. He stood for what he believed would make for the welfare of men. He taught, as a basic ethical principle, 'universal love'. He would have all men love one another as much as they loved themselves or their nearest of kin. He believed that if practised this would end war. He was immensely critical of war, but held that when waged in defence it was justifiable. He opposed as harmful the lavish burial ceremonies and extended mourning which were regarded as obligatory, and the elaborate ceremonial dances and the music which accompanied them. In contrast with the Confucianists, who argued that men's course is determined by fate, he stoutly maintained that men have free will. His followers separated into at least two schools, one stressing his religious beliefs and ethical precepts, working hard and living simply, and the other developing the logic which they found in his teachings.

Still another school which was developed in the long Chou era was that of the Legalists. It arose rather late, when China was being torn by wars among the states. It despaired of achieving stability and order by the Confucian way of a good moral example which postulated the basic goodness of human nature. It was also critical of the 'universal love' of Mo Ti. It insisted that what was needed was a body of laws, regulatory of imperfect human nature and impartially administered.

It was the Legalists, or School of Law, which at first seemed to succeed. As the central authority of the Chou Wang declined and as the culture associated with the Chou expanded over more and more of what we have called China proper, the wars between the states which made up the China of that time were intensified. Indeed, this stage of China's history is known as that of the Contending States (*Chan Kuo*). In the course of the struggle one state, Ch'in, with its centre in the north-west, emerged triumphant. It subdued its rivals and erased the last feeble remnants of Chou power. This last was in either 256 B.C. or 249 B.C. Ch'in had been organized according to the principles of the Legalists and seems to have owed its victory partly to this fact.

The undisputed dominance of Ch'in was short, from the defeat of its last rival in 221 to 206 or 202 B.C. Yet it was decisive. These brief years saw the culmination of a revolution from which emerged what in several ways was a new

China. Some have maintained that it was through the Ch'in that the Chinese Empire really arose. It is significant and fitting that our word China, by which the land is now known, is from Ch'in. Certainly the Ch'in ruler believed that he was making a new beginning. In contrast with the title Wang, which the Shang and Chou monarchs had borne, he adopted a title, Huang Ti, and called himself the first (Shih) to bear it. He is thus known to history as Shih Huang Ti, or, to prefix it by the name of the state, the designation also given to the dynasty which he inaugurated, Ch'in Shih Huang Ti.

How much of Shih Huang Ti's achievements were due to him and how much to his chief minister, Li Ssŭ, has been debated. Certainly they would have been impossible without the foundations laid by earlier rulers and ministers of Ch'in. Shih Huang Ti mastered not only his rivals in what then might be called China, but also extended his domains along the south coast into what was later called Indochina, a region which until then had been outside the circle of Chinese culture. He applied to all China the Legalist system which had been adopted in Ch'in. As had been true in Ch'in, the land was distributed among those who cultivated it, a process which was to be repeated more than once in later centuries, notably by the Communists in the mid twentieth century. He sought to eliminate the last traces of the states which had long been a divisive element and to end the debates between the several philosophic schools, for these might weaken the Legalism on which his rule was built. He had the arms of his former rivals melted down, reserving weapons to his own armies. He stopped the discussions of non-Legalist scholars with their criticisms of his regime and ordered the books on which they relied to be burned, exempting only a few categories and copies which were to be preserved in the imperial library. Through a system of roads he attempted to tie his realms to his capital, near the present Hsian, in the original territories of the Ch'in. A new style of script was promoted to make the writing of the Empire uniform and thus foster unity. To defend the Empire on its most vulnerable frontier, the north, Shih Huang Ti had the Great Wall constructed. It was not entirely a fresh creation, but took advantage of earlier barriers built by the individual states.

When, in 210 B.C., death removed the strong hand of Shih Huang Ti, the dynasty which he had so hopefully founded did not long survive. Revolts broke out, in part reactions against his radical, autocratic measures and protests against the distress brought by the vast expenditures and the conscription of labour entailed in his gigantic building enterprises. The regime collapsed in a welter of murders and civil strife.

The Ch'in Dynasty was succeeded by the Han Dynasty, inaugurated by a general of lowly birth who emerged as master in the contest for power. With an interruption about the time of Christ brought by an ambitious magnate who attempted to supplant it with one founded by himself, the Han Dynasty ruled the Empire for a little over four centuries, from shortly before 200 B.C. to A.D. 220. It marks a distinct period in China's history. Contemporary with the founding and the heyday of the Roman Empire, its territories were probably fully as extensive as the land area of that realm. It was not as populous, and it may not have been as wealthy as the Roman domains, but it had a high and creative civilization. With the one exception of the Roman Empire, no other state of its day equalled it in power, prosperity, and geographic extent. The Han Empire embraced all of China proper except the south-west, and at one time or another it also included what were later South Manchuria, North Korea, much of Sinkiang, and part of Indochina.

The outstanding monarch of the Han was Wu Ti, who was on the throne from 140 B.C. to 87 B.C., or a little over fifty years. Under him military operations greatly expanded the territories of the Empire – to the north-west into the later Sinkiang, to the north-east into Korea, along the south coast into what is now Indochina, and to a certain extent in the south-western mountains and plateau, the later Yünnan and Kweichow. He undertook vast public works, exalted the power of the throne over local magnates, and had a state monopoly of iron and salt. Yet his ambitious programme brought financial difficulties and entailed heavy taxation and the debasing of the currency.

He whom Chinese historians have regarded as a usurper, Wang Mang, in the first century after Christ put himself on the throne and attempted to found a new dynasty. He entered upon a comprehensive economic reorganization of the realm. He abolished the huge landed estates, nationalized the land and divided it among the cultivators, altered the currency, endeavoured to fix prices, and instituted state loans at moderate rates of interest to those requiring them for productive enterprises and for funeral and sacrificial purposes.

Under the renewal of the Han after Wang Mang's downfall, Chinese territory was extended afresh into what was later Sinkiang and beyond it into Central Asia. Caravan routes to the west were thus controlled and trade along them flourished. The Pan family from which came the generals chiefly responsible for these conquests also provided China with some of its most notable historians.

In political structure and in culture the China of the Han was both a continuation of the past and made significant modifications and contributions. With some delay, it checked the threatened renewal of the partition of the Empire into states with hereditary rulers. To prevent this it began the recruiting of a bureaucracy through civil service examinations, a principle which, much elaborated by later strong dynasties, persisted into the twentieth century. In place of Legalism the Han made Confucianism orthodox and for part of its course the realm was dominated by great families who were committed to that school and whose wealth was based upon the land. The Legalists did not give way without a struggle, and records survive of lively debates between them and the Confucianists over political and economic theory and specific measures. It was a modified Confuciansim which triumphed, a Confucianism more theistic than the Confucianism of the Chou. It made much of impersonal forces, such as the elements *yin* and *yang*, the former roughly equated with the female and negative and the latter with the male and positive elements in the universe. It viewed the universe as operating through their interaction.

The Han scholars endeavoured to recover and edit the literature of the Chou which had been scattered or destroyed in the wars in which that period had come to an end, by the measures of Shih Huang Ti, and in the disorder that had accompanied and followed the collapse of the Ch'in. Sharp differences of major proportions arose between those who held to what were called the Old Texts, written in archaic characters but forgeries of the Han, and those who clung to the New Texts, genuine survivals from the past but recorded in a simplified form of the characters which, prevailing under the Han, become standard for succeeding ages. Fresh literature was composed in large quantities, some of it in philosophy and much of it historical. The latter included a voluminous and comprehensive account of China's past by Ssŭ-ma Ch'ien, who is regarded as China's greatest historiographer. It was to be continued from time to time down into the twentieth century as the Dynastic Histories, the standard but not the only mine of information for the course of the Chinese people, their state, their achievements, and their culture. Members of the Pan family were responsible for the first notable continuation of Ssŭ-ma Ch'ien's history. Literature was furthered by the invention of paper, which provided a less bulky and a cheaper form of its dissemination and which, incidentally, eventually spread to Europe, becoming the source of the manufacture of paper in the Occident.

A distinctive and notable art developed, some of it showing the influence of the Chou and the Shang, some of it inspired by contacts with peoples to the west, and some of it original.

By the end of the Han, of the schools of thought which

had flourished in the Chou, only Confucianism and Taoism survived. The latter was modified, prospered, and became the system around which centred a movement which for a time created a regime that made a bid for the Empire.

Contacts were had with foreign peoples. Trade was carried on indirectly with the Roman Empire, and Chinese silk, conveyed by way of the caravan routes that led from the north-west of China proper, became common among the wealthy of that realm. Contributions came to China from the outside. In its effects the chief of these was Buddhism. It made its way to China and gained adherents, but it did not at once attain the popularity which it was eventually to enjoy.

When, in the first half of the third century of the Christian era, the Han Dynasty went the way of its predecessor, there ensued more than three and a half centuries of disunion. Much of it was marked by internal wars, and the earlier portion, that of the Three Kingdoms, in the half century which followed the Han, became famous in Chinese romance. In it flourished a trio of China's most notable military heroes. For a brief time later in the third and early in the fourth century most of what we have called China proper was nominally under one ruling house, but even in that brief interval of unity non-Chinese peoples, 'barbarians' from the north, were making themselves masters of much of the land. In the fourth, fifth, and sixth centuries the Yangtze Valley and the south were under a kaleidoscopic series of Chinese ruling houses and the north was divided among a succession of states in which the monarchs were non-Chinese invaders. The period paralleled the decline of the Roman Empire and the invasion of the Mediterranean Basin by the barbarians from the north.

Under these circumstances Chinese culture offered less resistance to foreign influences than at any time until late in the nineteenth century. It persisted, but Confucianism lost the dominance which it had enjoyed under the Han.

Buddhism grew in popularity and became firmly established. It was furthered by missionaries from abroad and by Chinese pilgrims who, having journeyed to the centres of their faith in India, returned, their enthusiasm heightened by what they had seen and heard. Buddhism brought much of the voluminous literature, including works of high philosophic and religious quality, which it had produced in the course of its pilgrimage, now of nearly a millennium, and great quantities of it were translated into Chinese. With it also came rich and varied art forms, some of them developed in Central Asia and North-West India under Hellenistic influences. It spawned sects, several imported and others primarily Chinese creations. Now, too, Taoism reached the apex of its popularity. It influenced Buddhism and was even more profoundly shaped by the foreign faith. It possessed a highly organized religious community made up of a majority who might be called the laity and of experts who constituted a minority. Its attraction was its promise of personal immortality, to be achieved by a varied regimen by which the physical body was transformed into one which was imperishable.

Other cultural developments there were – in literature, and in forms of writing. The drinking of tea, of southern origin, spread through the south and centre of China. Not until the eighth and ninth centuries did it become popular in the north. Eventually it played a large part in the life of China and was one of China's main contributions to the rest of the world. The invention of the wheelbarrow, a vehicle widely used on the narrow roads and streets which characterized the south and the Yangtze Valley, is also ascribed to the early part of this period.

The reunion of China was achieved by a dynasty, the Sui, in A.D. 589, but which, like the Ch'in eight centuries earlier, did not long survive its success. It was followed, in A.D. 618, by a dynasty, the T'ang, which ruled the Empire for nearly 300 years, until A.D. 907, one of the most glorious periods in the history of the Empire. In the early and more prosperous years of the T'ang, China embraced more territory and was probably more populous, wealthier, and more highly cultured than any other realm on the planet. In the seventh century its capital, Ch'ang-an, of which the present Hsian is a shrunken survival, was then almost certainly the largest city on the globe. From it the T'ang ruled an even larger area than had the Han. Its realms included not only all of China proper except the mountainous south-west, South Manchuria, and the later Sinkiang with its westward-stretching caravan routes, but also an alliance with a Korean kingdom which brought all that peninsula under its jurisdiction, and protectorates which included Afghanistan and the caravan cities in Central Asia and the valley of the Oxus.

Probably the ablest monarch of the T'ang was the second of the line to bear the imperial title. He is generally known as T'ai Tsung. He contributed markedly to his father's winning of the throne and to the firm establishment of the dynasty. On his father's abdication (627) he reigned in his own right until his death over two decades later (649). Under him Chinese rule was again extended into the Tarim basin and was pushed even farther westward, until the caravan cities Samarkand and Bokhara and much of the later Afghanistan and Russian Turkestan acknowledged his suzerainty. He strengthened the examination system for the recruitment of members of the bureaucracy. He emphasized Confucianism and ordered temples in honour of Confucius to be erected in every administrative subdivision of the realm. He fostered agriculture and commanded the re-establishment of public granaries in which stores could be accumulated in seasons of plenty for distribution in years when the crops were poor.

During the T'ang there lived and wrote the two men who are usually considered the outstanding poets of China, the bibulous, bohemian, and stylistically daring and original Li Po and, even greater as an artist and a genius, the conscientious Tu Fu, intimately acquainted with both beauty and tragedy and, like so many of the literary men of

China, with ambition and experience in the service of the state. Prominent also was Po Chü-i, who, living in the later turbulent years of the dynasty as a poet of the common people, was to be emphasized by the Communists in the twentieth century. Partly under the inspiration of Buddhism, painting flourished. It was then that one of the most famous of the many Chinese experts with the brush, Wu Tao-hsüan (or Wu Tao-tzŭ) lived and worked. Buddhism reached its apex and began the slow decline that marked its later course in China. Taoism was also popular. Significantly Confucianism revived and resumed the dominance which it had held under the Han and which it was to retain until the twentieth century. This was partly because it was deemed necessary to the state and partly because of the further development of the civil service examinations. These were largely based on the literature honoured by Confucian scholars, and this entailed its study in the schools through which preparation was made for them. Fiction, much of it tales long told by professional entertainers, was given written form in the vernacular. Printing made its appearance, apparently for the first time in the history of mankind, and later, combined with the use of paper which had come down from the Han, enabled the Chinese to multiply books beyond anything known elsewhere in the world until the nineteenth century. Partly through the elaboration of the civil service, the central government acted more directly on the masses of the people than formerly – a feature which was continued under subsequent dynasties.

The China of the T'ang had extensive contacts with other peoples and through them it both received and gave. Merchants came, some overland by the historic caravan routes and others by the sea. Foreigners of many peoples and cultures were to be seen on the streets of Ch'ang-an and in the ports on the south coast. Through them entered both Christianity and Islam, the latter faith then in the first stages of its amazing spread. However, both were represented only by small minorities and by the end of the T'ang

Christianity had disappeared. Chinese Buddhist pilgrims continued to make their way to the central shrines of their faith in India and to return with sacred books and enhanced zeal. Several food plants were introduced and enriched the Chinese diet. It was possibly then that the use of optical lenses was acquired from India. Chinese influences flowed outward, notably into Japan. The adoption and adaptation of Chinese culture by the Japanese, begun earlier, was now accelerated.

As had its great predecessors, the T'ang passed off the scene in a welter of rebellions and civil strife. These first assumed large proportions during the reign of him who is usually known as Ming Huang. Ming Huang was on the throne from 712 to 756, longer than any other monarch of the dynasty. Under him the T'ang reached its climax. In the West a military expedition carried Chinese arms into the upper reaches of the Oxus and the Indus. It was under him that Li Po, Tu Fu, and Wu Tao-hsüan (Wu Tao-tzŭ) flourished. But it was in his later years, when he became infatuated with one of the most infamous of China's beauties, that a rebellion broke out which caused him to flee from his capital and abdicate in favour of one of his sons. The revolt dealt the T'ang a blow from which it never fully recovered.

The disorder which followed the T'ang lasted for a little over half a century and was marked by five short dynasties. In 960 a new dynasty, the Sung, was founded by a successful warrior. It remained in power until 1279, or slightly longer than had the T'ang, but not as long as had the Shang, the Chou, and the Han. However, at no time did it control as much territory as had the Han or the T'ang. Its rule extended very little beyond China proper. Moreover, during the latter part of the Sung much of the north of China proper was in the hands of various alien conquerors. Yet the Sung was a period of striking cultural achievement. Porcelain and painting were notable. Printing was further developed and extant specimens witness to a superb technique. The printers aided the circulation of a voluminous literature, some of it old but much of it a fresh creation. Because of printing the reading public increased. Huge histories were written. Confucianism was re-formulated under Buddhist and Taoist influence with Chu Hsi as its outstanding synthesizer. That which emerged eventually became standard, and was accepted as orthodox until the twentieth century. Much attention was given to the civil service. The examinations which led to it were further developed. The state instituted and supported more schools which prepared for them. The professional civil servants took the lead in scholarship. Striking social experiments were undertaken which were associated with the programme of Wang An-shih and which included the monopoly of commerce by the Government and loans to farmers by the state at rates of interest which were much lower than could be had from private sources. Foreign commerce was attracted and much of it was by sea through the ports on the south coast.

In the thirteenth century the Sung succumbed to the Mongols, the first time that all of China had been mastered by foreigners. China was the richest and most populous part of an empire which stretched from the China Sea across the heart-land of Eurasia into what we think of as Russia, in area and probably in population the largest realm which until then had been brought under one rule. For a time the capital was at Cambaluc, approximately the later Peking. Foreigners from many nations and races entered the country, some of them as merchants and some employed by the Mongols. It was during Mongol times that the first Western Europeans reached China, some of them merchants, some missionaries, and at least one an engineer, the vanguard of the invasion which in the nineteenth and twentieth centuries was to work the most basic revolution that China had known. All of China proper was brought under Mongol rule, including the south-west, now for the first time fully incorporated in the realm. Through immigration and attendant conversions Islam gained the extensive foothold as an important minority which it has since retained.

In the fourteenth century the Mongol Empire broke into fragments. In China a rebellion which was partly nationalistic and anti-foreign swept out the Mongols. A new dynasty, the Ming, was founded by a successful general of humble origin who had once been a member of a Buddhist community. The Ming ruled China from 1368 to 1644. It was a period of prosperity, but it was shorter than that of the Han, the T'ang, and the Sung, and did not display as much cultural creativity and originality as had any of these three great predecessors. Its territorial extent was approximately that of the Sung, although it now included the south-west as the latter had not, but with one exception it did not reach out as successfully beyond the borders of China proper as had the Han and the T'ang. That one exception was fairly early in the dynasty, when formidable naval expeditions, under official auspices, semi-commercial and semi-political, went to South-East Asia, including Java, Sumatra, and Ceylon. They were not followed by the extension of China's rule, but they were significant as part of the movement of Chinese into that general area which attained increasing importance in the twentieth century. Ming painting and porcelain brought Chinese art to a new level of skill in technique. At first Nanking was the capital, but soon Peking was substituted for it, and it was at this time that Peking was given the great walls, temples, and palaces which in their main outlines persisted into the twentieth century and made it architecturally one of the most impressive cities of the world. Literature was produced and circulated in great quantities. Here and there fresh adventures were undertaken in philosophy and scholarship, among them one movement to get behind the Sung Neo-Confucianism to primitive Confucianism as seen in the Han editions of the works of the Chou period. However, in neither art nor scholarship were the Chinese doing or saying anything essentially new. In government they were perfecting the civil service examinations based on Confucianism, but this and the education which prepared for them tended to imprison the Chinese mind and outlook in patterns framed centuries earlier. Before the end of the dynasty, Europeans, led by the Portuguese and followed by the British and others, were again making their way to China by the sea routes, but they had little immediate effect on the Empire. The re-introduction of Christianity by Roman Catholic missionaries affected only infinitesimal minorities.

In the middle of the seventeenth century the Ming regime was terminated by foreign conquerors, the Manchus. Like the other invaders who had established themselves in China, they were from the north, the direction of chronic danger. As had the Mongols, after prolonged fighting they made themselves masters of all China, the second occasion in history that this had been accomplished by aliens. They remained in power until 1912. Thus for more than half the time after the Sung the Chinese were governed by foreigners. Here was a thought-provoking fact, fraught with implications for the future. Had the Chinese lost the ability to maintain their independence? As a qualifying consideration it must immediately be said that both Mongols and Manchus did not attempt to displace Chinese culture or Chinese institutions. They governed as native Chinese rulers had done and were regarded by the Chinese historians as in the legitimate succession to the dynasties. The Mongol Emperors had the dynastic title of Yüan and the Manchus that of Ch'ing.

The Manchus brought what we usually know as the Chinese Empire to its widest extent. Under them it included all of China proper and what we have called the outlying dependencies – Manchuria, Mongolia, Sinkiang, and Tibet. In addition several states were in a subordinate position which was without exact parallel in western international law. Of these the chief were Korea, Annam, Burma, and Nepal. Although this vast realm was gathered by the great Manchu Emperors, the Chinese regarded it as theirs and the regimes which succeeded the Manchus sought to extend their control over it – with the exception of Outer Mongolia, the recognition of whose independence was brought by Russian pressure, and of Burma and Nepal, which were never brought within the Manchu administrative system.

The first century and a half of Ch'ing rule was vigorous and under it the population of China rose to unprecedented proportions. Two reigns, known by the name of K'ang Hsi (1661–1723) and Ch'ien Lung (1736–96), covered most of that period and the Emperors who are usually remembered by those names were able and masterful. It was under them that the Manchu rule reached its greatest territorial dimensions. Population statistics for China are very uncertain, but the totals seem to have fluctuated greatly. During the prolonged internal strife which marked the end of the great dynasties they declined sharply, sometimes by as much as two-thirds. Yet until the Ch'ing they seem never to have been much above 100 millions. At the outset of the Ch'ing the total may have been 75 or 100 millions. By the end of the eighteenth century it had reached about 300 millions, and perhaps more. This means that it had multiplied between three- and four-fold in a century and a half. Why this was so we do not know. Although it appears to have begun in the later decades of the Ming, the increase may have been in part because of the strong government in the K'ang Hsi and Ch'ien Lung periods. Some have ascribed it to mounting food supply due to the introduction of maize, peanuts, and the sweet potato in the latter part of the Ming era and their rapid spread in the seventeenth century. The growth of population, continuing as it did in the nineteenth and twentieth centuries, although at not so rapid a rate, became one of the major problems of China.

In culture the China of the Ch'ing saw few innovations, but was largely a prolongation of that of the Ming. The Manchus continued to recruit the civil bureaucracy through the competitive examinations which were begun at least as early as the Han and were elaborated by the later major dynasties. Based as they were mainly on the classics esteemed by that school, they reinforced the hold of Confucianism on the Chinese. The Neo-Confucianism of the Sung remained orthodox. Literature was produced in vast quantities. With modifications, porcelain and painting were largely in the Ming tradition.

A feature of the great years of the Ch'ing was the continuation of the contacts with the Occident which had been renewed under the Ming. They were chiefly by sea and were deliberately restricted by the state. In the sixteenth century Portugal had acquired a foothold at Macao, a shallow harbour on a rocky island not far from Canton, and this she maintained. The Ch'ing attempted, and on the whole with success, to limit the sea-borne commerce to Canton and there to confine the foreign traders to a narrow strip along the river front outside the city wall, where were the 'factories', or places of business and residence of the merchants. True to the historic Chinese tradition, the Ch'ing refused to recognize any government as of equal rank with its own or to enter into the kind of diplomatic relations to which European governments had become accustomed in the family of nations which constituted the Western world. Before the Ch'ing had been in power many years the eastward expansion of Russia across Asia began to impinge upon the northern frontiers. Armed conflict followed, with a check to Russian southward advance into Manchuria. The resulting treaties (1689 and 1727) defined the boundary between the two empires, especially in the north-east, and provided for a limited overland trade and a semi-diplomatic Russian mission in Peking. Roman Catholic missions which had been renewed under the Ming were augmented under the first part of the Ch'ing regime. Jesuit representation at Peking was increased and the missionaries had charge of the mathematical and astronomical computations which regulated the official calendar. At imperial request they made maps of the realm, did paintings in European style, and supervised the erection of buildings in Western architecture at the summer palace. By the beginning of the eighteenth century there were between 200,000 and 300,000 Christians scattered through all but one of the provinces of China proper.

However, except for the possible contribution of the new

food plants from the Americas to the startling increase in population, the effect of the Occident upon China as a whole was very slight. A combination of factors prevented an increase in the number of Christians in the eighteenth century, and at the dawn of the nineteenth century Christianity seemed again to be dying out. Foreign merchants and trade were still closely restricted, and efforts from the West, notably from Great Britain, to establish continuing diplomatic relations after the European manner were rebuffed. China was the most populous empire on the face of the globe. Serene in their conviction of self-sufficiency and cultural superiority, the ruling classes wished to hold at arm's length the troublesome 'barbarians' who came by way of the sea.

The reverse effect, that of China upon Europe, was more marked. Many in Europe, especially among the intellectuals, warmly admired China. Gardens, pagodas, and pavilions were built after the Chinese style; lacquer, incense, and the Chinese manner of painting were popular; sedan chairs came into use, wall-papers were imitations and adaptations of Chinese models; numbers of Chinese plants and flowers were introduced; the drinking of tea became general, and the fashionable deism was reinforced by what was known of Confucianism, esteemed as that was as an example of the 'natural religion' which the deists prized in opposition to 'revealed religion'.

By the end of the eighteenth century the Ch'ing rule was beginning to give evidence of the decline which had characterized the later stages of earlier Chinese dynasties. In the nineteenth century, with occasional partial recovery, this became progressively more marked. Monarchs of mediocre or inferior ability followed the Ch'ien Lung Emperor and in general the Manchus deteriorated. As we are to see, a reprieve, temporary as it proved, was won through the energy and initiative of outstanding Chinese. Yet, when pressure from the Occident began to mount steeply, as it did in the nineteenth century, China had the misfortune to be handicapped by the decadence of the Manchus, aliens who clung to the power won for them by their vigorous ancestors.

CHAPTER THREE

THE CULTURE WHICH FACED THE EXPANDING OCCIDENT

WHAT were the outstanding characteristics of the culture which developed during the course of the history which we have so briefly summarized? Can we discern in them reasons for the disintegration of that culture in the twentieth century under the impact of the Occident? To what extent, if at all, did attitudes associated with that culture persist and enter into the kaleidoscopic fabric of the China of the first half of that century? We must postpone attempts to answer these last two questions until we narrate the course and describe the main features of that impact. Here we must concern ourselves chiefly with the first of the questions. But as we endeavour to answer it we must be aware that it has a direct bearing on the other two.

First we must remind ourselves again that the Chinese regarded their culture as the highest civilization, the only normal one for mankind. Many of them thought of it as ideally universal, embracing all men, and it was very difficult for them to accept the world into which they were forced by the West in the nineteenth and twentieth centuries, with its several cultures, of which that of China was only one. It was intensely galling to have their civilization regarded as inferior by Westerners, as it was in the nineteenth century, and to feel themselves impotent to maintain their political and economic independence against the advancing Occident.

Next we must note that this culture had Confucianism at its heart. As we have suggested, other strains entered, some of them from the Chou, that longest period in the history of China and the one where the major schools of philosophy took form. Of them, the Legalists left a permanent deposit in political theory and practice and, even more, Taoism persisted as a continuing religion and as an influence, sometimes profound, in the conceptions and attitudes of millions. The major contribution from abroad was Buddhism. Its teachings, including its ethics, its beliefs about life beyond the grave, and its ritual, entered into the warp and woof of Chinese culture. Indeed, Buddhism, Confucianism, and Taoism are often said to have constituted the three religions of China. Islam counted several millions among its adherents, but these were a minority which was largely apart from the main stream of Chinese life. However, Confucianism as adopted by the Han was the most potent influence. While it was weakened in the political disunity which followed that dynasty for more than three centuries and with the mounting popularity of Buddhism, it by no means disappeared. It revived during the T'ang, was reformulated under the Sung, and thereafter until the twentieth century its supremacy was never seriously threatened.

To Confucianism were due in part or entirely a number of the prominent features of Chinese culture. Although in this its outstanding thinkers were divided, in the main Confucianism took an optimistic view of the nature of man. A summary of Chinese lore, which was impregnated with its spirit and which was long one of the basic texts committed to memory by every schoolboy, began with the affirmation that man is by nature good. While it was clearly recognized that in practice men depart more or less widely from their nature, it was held that, because of this fundamental quality, men respond to reason and to worthy example. Whether in the state or in personal relations, therefore, physical force, while believed to be at times necessary, was regarded as a lower way. In contrast, learning and the scholar were honoured. By learning was meant primarily that based upon the classics from out of China's past which were valued by the Confucianists. As rated in later centuries, the chief of these were *The Four Books* and *The Five Classics*. All were believed to be principally from the Chou and either to have been revered by Confucius and to have been the subject of his study and meditation or to incorporate his teachings.

Thus *The Four Books* were the *Analects* (*Lun Yü*), made up of
his sayings and of the memories of him cherished and recorded by his disciples; *The Book of Mencius*, primarily the
teachings of him who next to Confucius was most honoured
by the school; and two shorter essays whose titles are usually
translated *The Great Learning* and *The Doctrine of the Mean*,
expressing ideals which were esteemed as true to those of the
Master. *The Five Classics* we have already named in our brief
account of the Chou. The Confucian scholar made these
books a chief subject of study. He memorized much or all of
their texts. He quoted from them and sayings from them
gained wide currency outside scholarly circles. Scholarship
was revered. Even the printed page was held in respect: the
written characters were not to be desecrated.

True to Confucian ideals, the scholar who was expert in
them was in theory, and to a large extent in practice, given
first place in the social scale. In a sense, China was governed
by philosophers. Beginning at least as far back as the Han,
as we have noted, and especially during and after the T'ang,
civil officials were increasingly recruited through competitive examinations. To have won a degree in these examinations brought prestige to oneself, one's family, and one's city
or community. China has known as much fighting as has
any country. Armed revolts have punctuated China's history and have been met by naked force; every dynasty was
founded by a warrior who emerged as victor in the welter of
civil strife which accompanied the decay of each dynasty;
several of the dynasties extended their domains over non-
Chinese peoples by military operations. Yet in theory the
soldier was accorded the lowest rank in a society where Confucian principles ran current.

Reinforced and moulded by Confucian principles, the
family was emphasized. Of the 'five relations' which were
inculcated as primary in the social order, three, those of
father and son, husband and wife, and older brother and
younger brother, were within the family. Only one, that of
prince and minister, had directly to do with the state.
Family duties were placed very high on the scale of moral

values, and filial piety was a major virtue. The family was regarded as including the ancestors as well as the living, and reverence for the ancestors, both in ritual and in life, was of great importance. Property was often owned in common and in the case of many well-to-do families three or even four generations lived together in a large establishment of many rooms and courtyards. Begetting sons to carry on the family line was a prime duty. Partly for that reason marriages were not arranged by the young people themselves but by their elders, and normally the two most immediately concerned were not consulted. Large families, or clans, had ancestral halls or 'temples', in which were tablets to the deceased members and where family ceremonies and consultations were held. Where it was strong, the family – meaning by that the entire connexion in the male line – cared for its aged, destitute, and ill and provided for the education of its brighter boys. In a sense it gave unemployment insurance and sick and old-age benefits. Each member had an obligation to his relatives, even distant ones.

The family system had advantages not only for its members but also for the Empire. To the latter, and especially to the Confucian tradition, it made for stability. Civil strife might rend the country and dynasties might come and go, but the family persisted. Many professed to be able to trace their lineage in unbroken known line to the Chou. In practice loyalty to the family took precedence over loyalty to the state. It was a matter of moral obligation to see that the members of one's family were supported, even though this might be at the expense of the government. The elders saw to it that the oncoming generations were indoctrinated with the traditional customs and ethics, and in these Confucianism predominated.

Yet the Chinese family also brought problems to society. Often it weakened the state by favouring for official posts men whose chief claim to office was their family connexions and whose appointment was pushed by influential relatives. This took place in spite of the system of competitive examinations, which in theory and to some degree in actuality were open to all and brought forward the most competent. Moreover, by placing a premium on male progeny the emphasis on the family gave a stimulus to population and tended to make the latter outrun the food supply.

Politically, as we have noted, the Chinese had a profound conviction, regarded as axiomatic truth, that civilized mankind – and by that they meant those who conformed to Chinese culture – should be under one government. In this they were reinforced by Confucianism. From time to time, as we have also seen, the country was divided among several ruling lines, once for more than two centuries. Yet this was regarded as abnormal and always the territory occupied by the Chinese was reunited. The Chinese were politically, socially, and historically minded. No other people has had a record of bringing together under one regime and set of institutions so large a population and so wide a territory over so long a period of time.

Chinese history did not fit into the categories familiar in the recent Occident, of 'ancient', 'medieval', and 'modern'. As the preceding chapter has disclosed, it was marked by a succession of dynasties. In general the pattern was fairly uniform. Into it entered economic, political, philosophical, and religious factors. A successful warrior made himself master of the Empire and began a new dynasty. After the Han this entailed no drastic change in structure. With modifications, some of which were notable, the laws and institutions of the preceding dynasty were continued. The Han had adopted Confucianism as the basis for the state, and it was this type of monarchy, built on Confucian principles, which persisted into the twentieth century. Under the vigorous rule of the founder of a major dynasty and his immediate successors, a degree of internal peace was achieved, the land prospered, wealth was accumulated, and population mounted. As the population multiplied the pressure on subsistence became more intense. At the same time the quality of the ruling house declined and through the process of heredity by which the imperial succession was determined men of inferior ability and character came to the throne. Because much depended on the Emperor, the administration deteriorated and proved unable to cope with the economic problems brought by the rising population. Rebellions broke out. Since, according to the Confucian theory, economic distress, government weakness, and natural disasters were laid at the door of the rulers, public opinion held the dynasty responsible and declared that it had lost the mandate of Heaven. Rebellions were accompanied by civil strife. When this was prolonged the economic fabric suffered, population fell off, and the pressure on natural resources was eased. In time one of the insurgents eliminated his rivals, including the reigning house, and put his family on the throne as a new dynasty. For the time being the problem of livelihood proved manageable as able administration brought internal peace and facilitated prosperity. Then the population once more multiplied, the quality of the Emperors slumped, and the cycle was repeated. Under each dynasty, especially under those with longer tenures of power, distinctive developments in culture were seen. In our rapid survey we have hinted at some of the chief of these. Chinese history, therefore, including that of Chinese civilization, falls into periods which are determined by dynasties. Yet always and increasingly Confucianism persisted as a continuing and controlling undercurrent.

This culture, which was so largely Confucian in its governing ideals, had both strength and weakness, strength and weakness which apparently were inherent. Its strength was in the emphasis upon the achievement of an ideal society, the sense of obligation to society which it inculcated, its emphasis upon intelligence and high moral character, and the relative stability which it gave to the family. The political structure which was developed was fairly well adapted to those ideals. It succeeded in holding together for several long periods the area in which the Chinese lived and gave to it cultural unity. At the top was the Emperor, and under him was a bureaucracy through which the Empire was governed both in its central offices and on the provincial and local level. The members of that bureaucracy were recruited, as we have seen, through competitive examinations which were more and more based upon the Confucian classics and which were designed to bring to the service of the state the most competent as judged by their proficiency in these classics, and thus in the basic convictions on which the Empire rested. Officials recommended protégées to the throne and were held accountable for their performance. On the level of the village and the clan there was much self-government, but, especially under and after the T'ang, subject to the supervision of a graded officialdom which was headed by the Emperor and the administrative bodies at the capital which were under his immediate direction.

The weaknesses of Chinese culture were many and helped to account for the collapse in the twentieth century under the impact of the West. The examination system and the education which led to it fostered memory and formalized literary style, but discouraged independent thought and did not disclose or nourish administrative ability. It was perhaps for this reason that after the Sung less and less that was new appeared, and that for more than half the time the Empire was ruled by alien dynasties which had seized the throne through conquest. To be sure, these dynasties, the chief of which were those of the Mongols and the Manchus, were regarded as in the legitimate succession, governed through institutions inherited from their Chinese predecessors, did not attempt to supplant Confucianism and its culture, and even, at least in the case of the Manchus, championed it. Yet, committed to this static culture and in the nineteenth century governed by an alien dynasty, which by an unhappy but not causally related coincidence became progressively decadent as the pressure from the Occident mounted, the Chinese were ill prepared for the new age into which they were hurried.

Moreover, in contrast with the traditional Chinese low rating of the warrior, the West traditionally honoured the soldier and was skilled in military and naval equipment and operations. It was therefore able by arms to impose its will on China. Even more significantly, and in striking contrast with the historic China, Western civilization was dynamic, and in the nineteenth and twentieth centuries was in revolution through processes and ideas which had been generated within it. The processes were associated with the development and application of the natural sciences and were displayed in the machine, the industrial revolution, and the mechanization of society. In contrast the Chinese had not developed what the Occident knew as the scientific approach. Why they had failed to do so has often been discussed, but no answer has been generally accepted. The Chinese displayed skill in some inventions – among them the compass, gunpowder, paper, printing, and methods of conserving the fertility of the soil – but they had not developed the scientific method nor achieved the skill in mathematics and in the development of the machine as they were seen in that Occident which forced itself upon them. Neither, for that matter, had any other culture outside the Occident. In the West there was also the ferment of Democracy, Socialism, and Communism. Moreover, in the West, in spite of growing departure from it on the part of many, Christianity, long the professed and dominant religion, was displaying enormous vigour, was giving rise to new movements, and was reaching out in an effort to bring its witness to all mankind.

Compared with other pre-industrial cultures, China's economic life was highly developed. As we have seen, by the dawn of the nineteenth century it was supporting a population of at least 300 millions. This was more than all of Europe or all of India, and perhaps than all the rest of Asia. Of course it was much more than that of all the Americas of that day or all of Africa. Indeed, it exceeded the combined totals of Africa and the Americas of the eighteenth century. The population of China was predominantly rural. Wealth was primarily in land. There were millions of peasant proprietors, but there were also millions of tenant farmers. The well-to-do might have some of their possessions in merchandise, shops, buildings, handicrafts, the precious metals, and a form of banking akin to pawnshops, but in general they sought to acquire or hold land and to draw their income from rents. There were thousands of towns and small cities, hundreds of them walled for protection. A few of the cities were large and probably had more inhabitants than any in the West of the eighteenth century. This meant numerous industries, but in the form of handicrafts largely organized by guilds and not stock companies. The Chinese were industrious and many of them displayed marked ability as merchants. Theirs had long been a money economy. In the nineteenth century coinage was largely in copper, but silver circulated in privately moulded bars. Moreover, China had had extensive experience with paper money, with its record of inflation.

The family, the state, the village, and the guild by no means exhausted the Chinese forms of organization. Secret societies were numerous and membership in them was widespread. Some had political purposes and were hostile to the existing dynasties. Several of the most notable rebellions had been spear-headed by them. Others of the societies were more for fellowship and for the mutual aid and support of their members.

The art of China was distinctive. Across the centuries many influences had entered from abroad and from several other cultural centres. The chief of these were through Buddhism, and therefore mainly from India, but also some were from Central Asia and even, via North-West India and Central Asia, from Greece. Whatever its origin, on all their art the Chinese impressed their distinctive genius. Especially notable were their achievements in bronze, painting, architecture, gardens, textiles, statuary, and ceramics, particularly porcelain. With the Chinese calligraphy was a fine art akin to painting. Before the nineteenth century, through paper, silk, tea, and porcelain, the Chinese had made contributions of great importance to much of the rest of mankind.

Though the vernacular was one of a family of tongues in East Asia, the Chinese language was almost in a class by itself, for it had developed after its own fashion. Several dialects were found, some of them, especially along the South

Coast, mutually unintelligible. However, the majority employed as the vernacular what Anglo-Saxons came to know as Mandarin. In one or another of many varieties, all of them reciprocally intelligible, this was the speech of almost all those in the north of China proper and in most of the Yangtze Valley and of the south-west. Its standard was that spoken in the capital, Peking, and it was therefore known as *kuan hua*, or the official speech. The language was written by means of characters, some of which went back to forms in use at least as early as the Shang. These characters were in part from conventionalized pictures of objects or ideas, in part were compounded of other characters, and to a large degree had phonetic origins. The literary styles developed by scholars were in use throughout the country, regardless of the vernacular, and helped to promote the cultural unity of the Empire. Through them, as we have seen, a voluminous literature was created. It was especially rich in poetry, history, philosophy, religion, and political, ethical, and social theory.

Much of the literature, notably the novel, was intended to entertain rather than to provoke thought. Moreover, the Chinese were very fond of the theatre. The theatre had conventions which seemed strange to the Westerner, but to the Chinese they appeared natural, and millions found their recreation in going to plays. Professional story-tellers had a numerous clientèle. Gambling was widespread: the Chinese were expert at games of chance. As a rule they did not engage in athletics or in sports requiring a combination of brawn and skill. They found their recreation in other ways. They had a keen sense of humour and knew that it lightened many a load. Yet it was not deemed proper to invoke it in such a way as to make another look ridiculous. 'Face' was important and the proprieties called for respecting it. It played a significant part in the diplomacy and the clash of cultures in the nineteenth and twentieth centuries.

Religiously the Chinese were a mixture. As we have repeatedly noted, Confucianism was dominant. It was optimistic about human nature, was highly ethical, and in general taught that the universe was friendly to man and made for righteousness. Its general trend was agnostic as to the existence of gods or God and the continuation of life after death. It looked with scorn on other religions and from time to time under its influence the state attempted to ban them. Yet in practice the great masses of Chinese were eclectic. They were at once Confucianists, Buddhists, and Taoists. While long in decline, in the nineteenth century Buddhism and Taoism were still potent and largely shaped the popular conception of what happens after death. Their pictures of heaven and hell were vivid. Buddhist monasteries were especially numerous. In Chinese religion there were additional elements. Some of these were from the remote past. Others were of recent origin. Belief in the existence and malign influence of evil spirits was almost universal. Animism of a primitive character flourished along with the more advanced faiths. There were many gods and cults of purely native origin. Except for Christianity and Islam, all religions tended to intermingle. At the outset of the nineteenth century Christians constituted a very small, widely scattered, and persecuted minority. Moslems were more numerous and were usually in distinct but tolerated communities.

Here was one of the major civilizations of mankind. It was the creation and the possession of what at the dawn of the nineteenth century was the largest fairly homogeneous group of mankind. While indebted to some other cultures, notably that of India, it was quite distinct, both from the other cultures of Asia and from that of the Occident. It could not be grouped glibly, as many from other areas, notably the Occident, were prone to do, under the classification 'Oriental'. It was as unlike the cultures of India and of Central and Western Asia as it was to that of the Occident. From it several of its neighbours had appropriated large elements. This was notably true of the Tibetans, Annamese, Koreans, and, especially, the Japanese. Yet in many ways it was a world by itself, almost as different as though it had been on another planet.

It was this culture which at the height of its geographic extent and of the numbers of people who conformed to it found itself invaded by that of another segment of mankind. The changes which followed were profound. It is that story which, as we indicated in the Preface, constitutes our major theme.

CHAPTER FOUR

THE PRESSURE OF THE OCCIDENT BEFORE THE REVOLUTION: THE NINETEENTH-CENTURY COURSE OF CHINA TO 1894

In the course of the nineteenth century the pressure of the Occident on China rapidly mounted, but it was not until the mid-1890's that the structure of Chinese culture really began to yield.

The pressure of the Occident on China was, as we have hinted, a phase of that expansion of European peoples and their culture which was one of the most striking features of the history of mankind in the nineteenth century. As we have seen, that expansion began long before the nineteenth century. As far back as the thirteenth century it had impinged upon China, but only fleetingly and without major consequences in that land. Contact was resumed in the sixteenth century, but China firmly restricted the commercial and religious activities of the Europeans. When, after the end, in 1815, of the wars of the French Revolution and Napoleon, Europe entered upon a period of relative peace which was not to be shattered until 1914, it greatly increased in wealth and population and its peoples pressed into all parts of the world. Seeking markets and raw materials for the factories which were multiplying as a result of the industrial revolution, they insisted that all other peoples open their doors to their commerce and for the investment of their surplus capital. Because of the revivals in Christianity, missionaries, both Protestant and Roman Catholic, multiplied and carried their faith to nearly every tribe and people.

Most peoples offered resistance but sooner or later all except some of the geographically inaccessible succumbed. In doing so, several, notably the Japanese, preserved their political independence. However, in the process they sacrificed their cultural independence. The Japanese, for

example, avidly adopted and adapted much from the
West. As a result, in the fore part of the twentieth century
the Japanese became one of the great powers of the earth.
In contrast, the Chinese attempted to hold the Occident at
arm's length and to preserve both their political and cultural independence. Accordingly they partly lost the first
and largely sacrificed the second.

The stepping up of the pressure of the Occident on China
began in the first decades of the nineteenth century. In spite
of the opposition of the imperial government, the numbers
of Christian missionaries began to grow. Roman Catholics
were able to smuggle in a few to reinforce their staffs, never
numerous, which had been sadly depleted by various
adverse circumstances in the preceding century. The first
Protestant missionary, Robert Morrison, under a British
society, arrived in 1807. He won a precarious foothold in
Canton. Others followed, some from Britain, some from the
United States, and at least one from the Continent of
Europe. So effective were the restrictions on their residence
and activities that, except for an occasional voyage along
the coast to distribute literature, Protestant missionaries
were confined to the foreign 'factories' on the river bank in
Canton and most of them established themselves among the
Chinese colonies under less unfriendly governments,
especially in Malacca, by that time under British rule, and
Bangkok.

It was commercial pressure supported by governments
and armed force which constrained the Chinese to open
their doors, at the outset by only a small crack. The initiative was British. This was to be expected. It was in Britain
that the industrial revolution began. For most of the
nineteenth century Britain led in the invention and pro-
duction of the new machines and in the development of
manufactures through them. For many decades after the
defeat of Napoleon the British mastery of the seas was not
seriously disputed. The British Navy dominated the oceans
and British merchants and British ships were in the fore-
front of the commercial penetration of the globe by Euro-

pean peoples. Continuing the growth that had been begun in the seventeenth century, the British Empire rapidly expanded until it became the most extensive of any that had been seen in all history. Under these circumstances British merchants would not be content with being as nearly excluded from China as they were at the outset of the nineteenth century.

To those concerned for British trade with China the conditions under which it operated were intolerable and became even more so as the years passed and the tide of British commerce mounted in other parts of the world. As we have seen, that trade, along with that of other Westerners, was closely restricted to one port, Canton. There it operated under conditions which to the foreigners were irritating in the extreme. Merchants from the Occident were permitted a barely tenuous foothold along the banks of the river outside the city wall. They were supposed to be there only during the season in which the prevailing winds made most convenient the arrival of foreign vessels. At other times in theory they were required to reside at the nearby Macao, which was still under Portuguese administration. The taxes of various kinds levied by Chinese officials on foreign ships and items of commerce seemed to the Westerners to be arbitrary and subject to unpredictable fluctuation. No direct contact could be had with the head Chinese officials. Intercourse was through a group of merchants known as the *Cohong*. By Chinese Government regulation, the *Cohong* possessed a monopoly on foreign trade and in return was held responsible for the foreign merchants. To Westerners, with their conceptions of a family of nations and of intercourse regulated by law and custom, the refusal of the Chinese to enter into diplomatic relations with other governments on the basis of equality seemed arrogant. To Chinese officialdom, with its conviction, long esteemed axiomatic, that all other states were inferior and peoples not accepting Chinese culture barbarians, Occidental demands appeared preposterous. Moreover, the fashion in which foreigners in China were handled by the courts and the Chinese laws and legal procedures so differed from those of the West that they seemed to Occidentals grossly unjust and were a chronic source of irritation. Here were two political systems and theories in irreconcilable conflict. One or the other must yield.

It was in the 1830's and 1840's that the issue first led to open war. Traditionally British trade with China had been a monopoly of the East India Company. Increasingly that monopoly was undermined, partly by employees of the Company who more or less surreptitiously engaged in trade on their own behalf, and partly by merchants who refused to respect the Company's legal rights and pressed into the Canton market. English cotton manufacturers were restive under what appeared to them to be the impediment placed by the Company's privileged position on access to the China market. It was chiefly they who persuaded Parliament (1834) to pass an act which ended the East India Company's monopoly of the China trade. The British Government appointed a succession of superintendents to reside in Canton and to supervise its citizens and their commerce in that port. Almost immediately friction arose between the superintendent and the Chinese officials. In accordance with their tradition the latter insisted on regarding him as a chief merchant and holding him responsible for actions of British merchants which appeared to them to be reprehensible. Moreover, the viceroy, the highest Chinese official in Canton, refused the request of Lord Napier, the first superintendent, to enter into direct relations with him, for, contrary to all Chinese convictions, this would acknowledge the equality of the British and Chinese Governments.

A crisis came over opium. Increasingly the drug, chiefly from India, had become the main commodity imported into China by Westerners. Opium-smoking was becoming a major vice. Its debilitating effects upon increasing thousands was of deep concern to the Chinese Government. Since because of its purchase the balance of trade was against China, officials feared that the country would be drained of its silver. Edicts against the smoking of opium and the importation of the drug availed little. The growth of the opium poppy in China itself increased and quantities of opium were smuggled in from abroad, not only through Canton but also through other ports. Late in the 1830's efforts to halt the trade and stamp out the use of the drug were intensified. The Chinese High Commissioner appointed to carry out the imperial will forced the surrender of the opium held by foreign merchants in Canton and insisted that foreign ship-masters undertake to bring in no more. As a result, in November 1839, hostilities broke out between the British authorities and the Chinese.

From the standpoint of the Chinese the cause was opium and the resulting struggle was remembered by them and by much of the rest of the world as the Opium War. From the British viewpoint opium was only incidental. The real grounds were the galling restrictions of the Chinese on foreign trade and the refusal of the Chinese to deal with British officials on the terms of equality which Occidentals deemed a concomitant of civilization.

The attack was pressed intermittently by the British forces, with fruitless attempts at a peaceful settlement. Finally, in August 1842, after the English had taken several ports, the Chinese yielded and a treaty was signed at Nanking. By the terms of the treaty, Hongkong, an island off the south coast not far from Canton seized during the course of the war, was ceded outright to Great Britain. In addition, five ports, Canton, Amoy, Foochow, Ningpo, and Shanghai, all south of the Yangtze, were opened to foreign residence and trade. The duties to be levied by China on that trade were fixed. The English were to appoint superintendents or consular officers in each of the five ports to be channels of communication between the merchants and the Chinese officials and to see that duties and other dues were paid by the merchants.

A few other Western powers, notably France and the United States, took advantage of the situation also to obtain treaties. Since 1784 Americans had engaged in trade with China and by the 1830's they were second only to the English in the dimensions of their commerce with that land. The same five ports were declared open to them, the appointment of consuls was specified, and the fixing of tariffs agreed upon. In addition the treaty with the United States contained what is generally known as extraterritoriality. By it Chinese subjects guilty of criminal acts against citizens of the United States were to be arrested and punished by the Chinese authorities according to the laws of China, while citizens of the United States who committed any crime in China were to be tried only by a consul or other public functionary of the United States and according to the laws of that country. The principle of extraterritoriality was extended to the citizens of the other powers having treaties with China.

By the treaties of the 1840s a more extensive trade was permitted with Westerners, the beginnings of official intercourse were regularized, and some of the procedures which had been sources of irritation were dealt with in a way which on paper went far towards satisfying the foreigner. Tariffs were now fixed and foreigners were no longer to be subject to Chinese criminal laws and procedures. Foreigners established themselves in the five ports, although not without friction, notably in Canton. On the island of Hongkong, now become a British crown colony, a thriving city arose. Trade mounted. Imperial edicts gave toleration to Christianity and both Roman Catholic and Protestant missionary activities multiplied.

Within a few years war again broke out. The existing treaties proved satisfactory to neither the Chinese nor the Westerners. To the former they seemed to grant too much, to the latter too little. Friction increased, particularly, as earlier, with the British, the people who, as heretofore, had the major share in the commerce. In 1856 it culminated in open fighting, at first near Canton. In an earlier stage of the war the foreign 'factories' at Canton were burned and thus the physical symbols of what had been an important stage of the Western impact upon China were erased. They had housed a compact community some of whose members looked back upon it with a kind of nostalgia. It was the prototype of other foreign communities which arose in the treaty ports. The French soon entered, initially in reprisal for the murder of a French Catholic missionary. Except for brief action in 1856, the Americans remained neutral. Yet they, like the English and the French, with the Russians, pressed China for a broadening of commercial and diplomatic relations. To bring the imperial government to time, naval action was carried to Tientsin, the port of the capital, Peking.

Thus pressed, the Chinese entered into negotiations and in 1858 they signed new treaties with Great Britain, France, Russia, and the United States. The British, French, and Russian treaties provided for the exchange of ratifications at Peking, and on the principle of 'the most-favoured nation' treatment contained in its treaty, the representative of the United States demanded a similar procedure. The Russians and the Americans peacefully obtained the specified exchange in Peking, but the latter were treated in the manner in which the Chinese had been accustomed to deal with other governments on the assumption that they had an inferior status. The English refused to consent to any measures which would be short of the exchange of ratifications in Peking or which would imply anything less than the full equality with the Chinese which had been written into their treaty. At first repulsed in their efforts to go to Peking by way of Tientsin, in 1860 they returned in force, took Tientsin, and occupied Peking. In retaliation for the violation of a flag of truce and what, from their standpoint and from that of Western international law, was the wanton imprisonment of representatives who were protected by it, the English burned the imperial summer palace west of Peking. Thus coerced, the Chinese authorities yielded and ratifications of the British and French treaties were duly exchanged in Peking. Two conceptions of relations between nations had again clashed. Westerners sought to impose theirs on the Chinese.

The latter, unconvinced, yielded to force and ostensibly acquiesced. However, they were confirmed in the conviction that they were dealing with uncivilized 'barbarians', successors of those who from time to time had conquered and occupied all or part of the Empire.

The treaties of 1858, usually known by the name of Tientsin, were important. With those of 1842–44 they formed the chief legal basis for relations between China and Western powers until well along in the next century. Not until the 1940's were they fully superseded. It was largely under them that the penetration of China by the Occident was accomplished.

The most significant of the terms of the treaties of Tientsin can be fairly quickly summarized. Diplomatic representatives were to be appointed to the court of the Ch'ing and might, at the option of their governments, either reside permanently in Peking or visit that city occasionally. They were not to be called upon to perform any ceremony derogatory to the status of their respective governments as fully equal to that of China and were to be assisted in acquiring property in Peking for the use of their representatives. Consuls were also to be appointed with the right of residence in any of the open ports. If they so chose, the Chinese might appoint diplomatic representatives to Western governments. Protection was promised Christian missionaries and their converts in the peaceable teaching and profession of their faith. When equipped with passports, foreigners might travel anywhere in the Empire. Foreign merchant ships were to be permitted on the Yangtze River and as many as three ports were to be opened to their trade as far up the river as Hankow. Several additional ports along the coast including Manchuria were opened to foreign residence, and one on Formosa. Extraterritoriality was reaffirmed. Detailed provisions were entered for the duties to be charged on imports and exports and the dues to be paid by ships. Under the most-favoured nation clause contained in the treaties, concessions granted to one country were automatically extended to all.

It will quickly be seen that under the treaties of the 1840's and 1850's China formally assented to the legal equality of other nations with herself, a principle quite new in her history. She did more. She consented to conditions which made her less than the equal of Western states. She freed the citizens of powers with whom she had treaties from the jurisdiction of her courts in criminal matters. She sacrificed her authority unilaterally to fix tariffs and agreed that these should be subject to agreement with foreign governments. Chinese Christians were in part put under the protection of foreign powers. Foreign ships were permitted to traverse the chief of her internal waterways. Some of the concessions were designed to remove friction, but they were chiefly to the advantage of Westerners and several of them were of a kind which Western powers would not permit in their relations with one another. Always they irritated the Chinese and in the next century the latter denounced them as 'unequal' and sought to be freed from them.

An ominous accompaniment of the war of 1856–60 was the delimitation of the eastern boundary between the Russian and Chinese Empires. By a treaty signed in May 1858, a few weeks before those signed in Tientsin with Great Britain, France, and the United States, China agreed that the territory north of the Amur River should be Russian and that that east of the Ussuri should be jointly occupied by the two powers. In 1860 China surrendered her claim to the latter area. Few if any Chinese had ever been in the regions thus defined as Russian or were residents there, and the Manchus seem never adequately to have occupied the territory. Yet the agreements marked a stage in Russian encroachments on land which was clearly part of the Chinese Empire and paved the way for even more spectacular increase of Russian influence late in the century and under Communism in the second quarter of the twentieth century.

Also as a portent, and in this case of the profound cultural revolution which was to issue from the impact of the Occident, was what was known as the T'ai P'ing Rebellion.

The T'ai P'ing movement had its rise through Hung Hsiu-ch'üan, the son of a farmer near Canton, a school teacher and a disappointed competitor in the civil service examinations. In an illness he had visions which he interpreted in the light of a set of pamphlets which, written by a Chinese convert, set forth the main tenets of Christianity as taught by early Protestant missionaries. He and a cousin baptized each other and he began to preach a faith which was compounded of inherited conceptions, his visions, and what he had learned from the Christian tracts. This was about 1843. For approximately two months in 1847 Hung received instruction from a Protestant missionary in Canton. From his preaching and that of his friends there arose, at first in the mountainous province of Kwangsi in the south, a movement which sought to overthrow the Manchus and to establish a new dynasty. To it was hopefully given the designation T'ai P'ing, 'Great Peace'. To the movement were attracted a number of dissatisfied elements and it was in part an agrarian revolt, one in a long succession in China's history. It differed from the others in its religious content, derived from Christianity and therefore from the West. It destroyed idols, it utilized a Protestant translation of the Bible, it had baptism and forms of worship which were in part adaptations from Christian sources, and it observed one day in seven for worship. It made much of the Ten Commandments and was sternly against the use of opium, alcohol, and tobacco. Yet it did not observe the Holy Communion and did not teach the cardinal Christian ethical principle, love. It advocated social and economic reforms, including the redistribution of land, but did little to carry them out. It was intensely Chinese and insisted that foreigners acknowledge the supremacy of Hung Hsiu-ch'üan as Emperor and as religious leader, for it claimed universality for its faith.

The T'ai P'ing movement gained temporary but destructive success. Fighting with the governmental forces broke out late in 1850. Owing to the weakness of the Manchu regime, and in part to their zeal and organization, the T'ai P'ing forces won considerable initial victories. Eventually they established themselves at Nanking and made that city their capital. They controlled much of the lower reaches of the Yangtze Valley. However, as administrators they were failures and a northern expedition which was aimed at Peking proved a fiasco. They took a fearful toll in lives. Hundreds of thousands perished. Much of the Yangtze delta was laid waste, and some of the best libraries were burned. Several Protestant missionaries viewed the T'ai P'ings hopefully but were disillusioned. Nor did the latter gain the support of Western powers.

The suppression of the T'ai P'ing Rebellion was mainly the achievement of Chinese who rallied to the support of the dynasty. Outstanding was the Confucian scholar Tsêng Kuo-fan, who, although with no previous military experience and learning by trial and error, recruited and directed forces which proved effective. Among other Confucian scholars associated with him who gained reputations as generals were Tso Tsung-t'ang and Li Hung-chang. Tsêng Kuo-fan and Tso Tsung-t'ang were natives of Hunan, in the south centre of China proper, the province from which was to come Mao Tse-tung, the outstanding Communist leader of the second half of the twentieth century. The imperial forces slowly reduced the T'ai P'ing armies. They received aid from foreign volunteers, the best known of whom was the British soldier, a kind of modern knight-errant, Charles George Gordon. Nanking fell in 1864, and by February 1866 the last of the insurgents, who had taken refuge in Hung's native province, were eliminated. For the time being the traditional order had triumphed. Indeed, the outstanding Chinese, reinforced by the experience in their conviction that what came from the Occident made for the destruction of civilization, may have been even more adamant against admitting the foreigner and his culture.

Some of the T'ai P'ings escaped and went overseas to the Chinese colonies outside the Empire. They helped to prepare the way for the revolutionary movement which swept China early in the following century. Many of the Chinese who shared in that movement looked back upon the T'ai P'ing revolt as the precursor of the later drastic changes.

In the 1860s several other rebellions, but none of them influenced by the Occident, threatened the existence of the dynasty. In the 1870s floods in the south and drought in the north brought distress. Particularly in the north, in 1877 and 1878 famine took a million or more lives. Indeed, for a time it looked as though the Manchus had sacrificed the mandate of Heaven. Defeat at the hands of Westerners, loss of territory to the Russians, revolt after revolt and natural disasters seemed to spell their doom. The throne was occupied by minors who followed incompetents. He who is known by his reign name, Tao Kwang, died in 1850 and was succeeded by a son with the reign title Hsien Fêng. The Hsien Fêng Emperor proved dissipated and died in 1861, still a young man and a refugee from his capital, occupied as that had been by British and French forces. His heir was an infant, who as he reached adolescence was dissolute and died in 1875, soon after having passed out of the control of a regency. Another infant followed him on the throne. Pressed from without and within, the Manchus appeared to be hastening to their end.

Yet the Manchus were given a reprieve. That was partly because many Chinese Confucian scholar-officials rallied to their support. To the latter the alternative seemed chaos and even the disintegration of the traditional culture which to them, reared as they had been, appeared to mean the end of civilization. As the main leader in the suppression of the T'ai P'ing Rebellion, Tsêng Kuo-fan was the outstanding statesman of the 1860s and until his death (1872). High-minded, honest, public spirited, able, he was a model of the Confucian scholar-official and out of conviction was wedded to the existing order. Tso Tsung-t'ang led in putting down one of the most serious of the other revolts, that in the north-west and in Sinkiang, and in doing so displayed marked resourcefulness. Towards the end of the century, although not the equal in integrity to his early patron, Tsêng Kuo-fan, Li Hung-chang came to the fore. There were other able Chinese in officialdom and not all the Manchus were degenerate.

The most picturesque Manchu of the second half of the nineteenth century was a woman, she who is best known as Tz'ŭ Hsi, and to Westerners as the Old Buddha or the Empress Dowager. Born in 1835, of a good but not distinguished Manchu family, she was chosen as one of the low-ranking concubines of the Emperor who is best known by his reign title, Hsien Fêng. She bore him his only son. The Hsien Fêng Emperor died in 1861, as we have seen, while a refugee in Jehol, the imperial country seat north of the Great Wall. Her son, still a young child, succeeded to the throne under the reign title of T'ung Chih. She soon adroitly seized the real power, eliminating the regents appointed by the will of the Hsien Fêng Emperor and having herself and the latter's first wife designated Empresses Dowager and then regents. Since she was abler and more forceful than her colleague, she became the most important person in the central administration. Early in 1875, soon after his marriage and nominal assumption of control, her son died, ostensibly of smallpox, and without a son, although his wife was then with child. Tz'ŭ Hsi thereupon insisted on the elevation of another infant to the throne, he who is best known by the title of his reign, Kuang Hsü, and she and the other Empress Dowager again became regents. This step was contrary to the dynastic law of succession, for the new Emperor was of the same generation as his predecessor and therefore could not be posthumously adopted as the latter's son and engage in the rites which custom required of one in that position. In spite of protests and the suicide of the late Emperor's widow before the birth of her child, Tz'ŭ Hsi carried through her purpose. The illness (1880) and death (1881) of her co-regent left Tz'ŭ Hsi sole regent and the real ruler of the Empire. After several years (1889) she married her niece to the young Emperor and theoretically retired, but actually kept her hands on affairs of state. Using funds which had been designated for the building of a modern navy, she had constructed as her residence a summer palace, set in extensive and elaborately landscaped grounds. We are soon to meet her again, for she remained the dominant figure in the Manchu regime until her death (1908). She possessed prodigious physical vitality, had unbounded ambition, and was both skilful and masterful in her manipulation of men and of the machinery of the central administration. She had a wide knowledge of Chinese literature, was fairly competent in the Chinese documentary literary style in which state papers were drafted, and was proud of her calligraphy. She was superstitious, avaricious, quite unscrupulous in her methods of obtaining money and power, at some crucial times was vacillating and irresolute, and until her later years, and perhaps even then, failed to appreciate the significance of the forces which were playing upon China from the outer world. In her prime she may have prolonged the life of the dynasty, but this she was able to do only because of the co-operation of outstanding Chinese. In the end she hastened its downfall and was partly responsible for the disorder into which its passing plunged the country.

As we have suggested, breathing space was won for the Empire by the treaties of 1858 and by the suppression of the rebellions of the third quarter of the century. Had the Chinese and Manchu leaders possessed the wisdom of their contemporaries in Japan they might have used it to prevent the collapse of the old order and the near approach to anarchy which followed it. In these same years the Japanese, as we have noted, from an even more resolute isolation from the Occident, guided by astute men, were seeing the impossibility of maintaining that policy and were rapidly adopting and adapting from the West what seemed to them of value. They introduced the mechanical appliances and science of the Occident, built factories, constructed railways, reorganized their army and navy on European models, created a new currency and banking system, began a merchant marine, telegraph lines, and a postal network, framed a constitution with a diet or parliament and a cabinet partly dependent upon it, and developed an educational system which copied much of what they found in Europe and the United States. They did this without jettisoning their basic institutions. They preserved their family traditions, kept and even strengthened the historic position of the Emperor and the Shinto cult by which it had been reinforced, and conserved the prominence of the military while broadening its base and adopting the weapons and the methods of the Occident. Outwardly revolutionized, Japan made the transition into the modern world without the sharp break with her past that was to characterize the China of the twentieth century.

During these years of golden opportunity and in contrast with Japan, China sought to remain as little altered as possible. This was probably to have been expected. While jealously guarding their political independence, the Japanese had been accustomed to taking over from other peoples what seemed to them of value. Especially had they borrowed from the Chinese, and to such an extent that in many ways their culture was a variant of that of China. On the other hand, the Chinese, while from time to time submitting to foreign rule, had regarded their civilization as superior to all others, and for the most part their conquerors had either adopted that civilization or had permitted it to continue altered but little if at all. The Chinese had accepted some contributions from other peoples, notably Buddhism, but without seriously impairing their inherited culture. Their neighbours had imitated them far more than they had imitated their neighbours. Not unnaturally, in view of the fashion in which they had forced themselves upon China, the sea-borne invaders were regarded as barbarians. The Chinese were, therefore, determined to have as little to do with them as possible. The scholar-officials, the *literati*, who were the leaders of the Chinese and the historic exponents and guardians of Confucian culture, were particularly adamant in their resistance to Occidental ways. The Manchus, seeking to hold the control which was threatened by their own decadence and incompetence, were even less disposed to yield.

In spite of this unwillingness to learn from the Occident,

in the slightly more than a third of a century which followed their second war with Great Britain the Chinese here and there began to bow to the inevitable and to make some adjustments to the Occident. Late in the 1870's the Chinese Government established legations in London, Washington, and several other capitals in the Occident. It was thus accepting diplomatic intercourse on the basis of equality between states. At least two schools were inaugurated, also under the government, to train young men for the diplomatic service. In the 1870's, moreover, the government sent over a hundred boys to the United States for education. This was at the instance of Yung Wing, who had been educated in a Western fashion by Protestant missionaries and had been sent by them to the United States to complete his training in a secondary school and university. Through foreign residence and travel he had become convinced of the necessity of providing that opportunity to others if China were not to stumble blindly in the new age into which she was being hurried. Conservatives, alarmed at what they deemed the deculturalization of the students through foreign residence, had the enterprise discontinued, but several of those prepared through it later had significant parts in essaying adjustments of their native land to the Occident. Some became officers in the navy that was being built on foreign models, some were in the telegraph service, some aided in the railways and mines, a few were in business, and a few in the consular and diplomatic service. As may be gathered from the last sentence, beginnings were being made in introducing several Occidental appliances. Here and there arsenals were erected to supply China with Western-style arms and ships, for some officials were convinced that only thus could the threat of Western fleets and armies be met. By the mid-1890's a few railways were being planned and beginnings made towards construction. The government built telegraph lines to aid it in its functions. The China Merchants Steam Navigation Company was organized for purposes indicated by its name. At least one coal-mine was opened after the manner of the Occident. An occasional technical school was conducted to train men for these new ventures.

Yet these were exceptions. In general the government remained in the hands of those educated after the Confucian manner and committed to the traditional ways. As yet the Chinese, whether the rank and file or the dominant classes, were unconvinced of the need of radical change.

Pressure and penetration from the Occident continued through several channels. In the ports which were opened to foreign residence and trade communities of Westerners arose. So far as they were composed of merchants and consuls, as in most cities they predominantly were, in their social life they tended to keep aloof from the Chinese. Few of them learned Chinese or knew much about Chinese culture. For communication with the Chinese they generally used what was called pidgin English. This had a vocabulary which was mainly derived from English, but it also contained words of other origins. In sentence structure it showed the influence of the Chinese language. Foreign merchants usually carried on their business with Chinese merchants through what were called compradors. These were Chinese in their employ who knew English or pidgin English. The foreign communities were often in special districts of the ports, denominated settlements or concessions. Since, under extraterritoriality, in criminal cases they were not subject to Chinese law, but were under such courts as their governments set up, it was more convenient for foreigners and for the Chinese authorities to have them segregated. Some of the concessions provided such public services as police, streets, water, sewage, and lighting. They were bits of the Occident set down in China.

The largest of the foreign communities was in Shanghai. At the time when the first treaties made it an open port, Shanghai was of minor importance, an insignificant walled city on a small stream which emptied into the mouth of the Yangtze. Because it was near the mouth of the largest of China's rivers, in time it became the chief port of China. The heart of its business district and a large proportion of its foreign residences were in what was called the International Settlement. This was made up of the British and American concessions and, although the majority of the residents eventually were Chinese, it was governed by a municipal council of foreigners elected by the foreign land-renters. Adjoining the International Settlement was the French Concession, under its own municipal council.

In most of the other ports the concessions of the various treaty powers, while adjoining one another, remained distinct, each under its own consul. Peking was not a treaty port, but most of the foreign legations were in a section next to the south portion of the vast wall which guarded the city.

A further development in the decades following the treaties of 1858 was the creation and growth of the Imperial Maritime Customs Service under foreign direction. The customs duties, as we have seen, were fixed by treaty. Their collection became a problem. It became especially acute at Shanghai in the 1850's, when the disorders attendant on the T'ai P'ing Rebellion made difficult the operation of the machinery which had been set up to solve it. A plan was there devised for collection under the supervision of foreigners appointed with the concurrence of the Chinese Government. The method then improvised proved so satisfactory to both Chinese and foreigners that it was continued and elaborated and was extended to other ports. An agreement of 1858 provided for a system which would be uniform for all the ports and for the appointment of foreigners to assist in it. It was given a comprehensive organization under an official known as the Inspector-General of Customs. In 1863 this post was given to an Irishman, Robert Hart, who held it until his death (1911). After 1908, however, he was on leave in England and the active direction of the service was in other hands. Before he was given the office, much had been done by his predecessors to put the Customs Service on a sound basis. Under Hart's able and long direction the service was greatly enlarged and assumed more and more functions. Its higher ranks were held by Westerners, predominantly British. Officials of the Chinese Government, for the most part they were men of integrity who were examples of honest and competent administration in a land where under a declining dynasty dishonesty and incompetence in the government were rife. As more ports were opened to foreign residence and trade the Customs Service extended its operation to them. In several ports the natives customs in the vicinity were put under it. It built lighthouses, placed and attended buoys and beacons, supervised harbours, charted coasts and rivers, took quarantine measures, made meteorological observations, gave out storm warnings, and in other ways aided navigation. It issued reports on trade. In 1896 Hart was put in charge of the Imperial Postal Service, and it was so expanded that in 1911 it was removed from the supervision of the Customs Service and made independent. Hart was the trusted adviser of Chinese officials in many matters of state, including especially foreign relations.

Increasingly foreign steamers plied the coastal waters and the chief rivers of China, notably the Yangtze and its tributaries.

In commerce, in the foreign communities in the ports, and in much of Chinese relations with the powers Britain was predominant. As we have seen, British initiative was responsible for the opening of China. British leadership created the Customs Service. Great British firms had houses in several of the ports and maintained steamship services. The Hongkong & Shanghai Banking Corporation, a British institution, was the leading foreign bank and had branches in several ports. The *North China Daily News* and its weekly edition, the *North China Herald*, both published in Shanghai and both British, were the chief reliance of the foreign communities for news. An American, Anson Burlingame, led the first Chinese diplomatic mission abroad (late in the 1860's), but it was in London that the first of the Chinese legations in the Occident was set up in 1877. American shipping, which had been large in the first half of the century, sharply declined in the 'seventies and left the British supreme.

Yet foreign trade mounted but slowly. Between 1865 and

1885 it increased only about a fifth. In the next decade it nearly doubled, but by 1895 Chinese economy went on almost as though it were non-existent. In 1895 cotton goods, chiefly from Lancashire, were the chief import, with opium second. The leading exports were tea and silk, but both were beginning to suffer from the competition of other lands. More and more the Occident was buying tea from India, Ceylon, and Java, and silk from Japan and the Levant. Except for cotton goods, and perhaps tea, both imports and exports were luxury items.

One form of penetration from the Occident which by 1895 had reached all the provinces and the fringes of the outlying dependencies was through the Christian missionary. Both Roman Catholics and Protestants largely increased their missionary staffs. Under the treaties of 1858 Christian missionaries were legally permitted to travel and preach anywhere in the Empire. Both in the treaty ports and in many places outside these ports they acquired property and established residences. Roman Catholics were almost entirely from the continent of Europe, mainly from France. In 1897 they numbered a little more than 750. Chinese Roman Catholics were now slightly more than half a million, an increase of about two-and-a-half-fold since the dawn of the century. Protestant missionaries increased from about 189 in 1864 to nearly 1,300 in 1889. They were mostly from the British Isles and the United States, with the former leading, especially through the undenominational China Inland Mission, British founded and led, which in 1895 had over 600 representatives in China. The total of Protestant communicants rose from about 5,700 in 1869 to about 55,000 in 1893.

Compared with the vast population of China, these figures are not particularly impressive. However, they are evidence of an influence far greater than bare enumeration reveals. They represented not only a religion which was dynamic. They also were often accompanied by political pressure, particularly from the French Government, which insisted upon a protectorate over Roman Catholic missions and used it to enhance its position in China. Even more, Christian missions, especially those of Protestants, became channels for several features of Occidental civilization. Protestant missionaries were the chief pioneers of Western medicine and surgery. These were making remarkable advances in Europe and America and missionaries were bringing them to bear upon disease in China. Missionaries were founding schools in which Western learning was taught, the main forerunners of the educational revolution which was to come. The Bible was translated and widely circulated. Several books on Western history and international law were translated or written and helped to broaden the horizon of their readers. With the purpose of relieving famine and disease and improving living standards, efforts, as yet limited, were put forth to acquaint the Chinese with the methods and fruits of Western science. Still more significant was the fact that for those Chinese who adopted the faith, Christianity displaced other religions, especially Confucianism. Here was a force which if it became dominant would work a basic revolution, destroying the ideological foundation on which Chinese culture rested. It was not adopted by a sufficient number to effect of itself that revolution. Moreover, many missionaries wished to preserve such of Confucianism as was not clearly contradictory to Christianity. Yet in Christianity and its missionaries there was that which weakened Confucianism and which contributed to its eventual passing.

The presence of foreigners, and especially of missionaries, for the latter made their way into the interior to a greater degree than did merchants and diplomats, aroused resistance. Much of this was from the officials and the intellectuals, jealous guardians of Chinese culture. Some of it spread to the masses and from time to time led to antiforeign riots.

Emigration of Chinese, chiefly labourers, was a frequent source of friction. Much of it, especially to sugar and guano estates in the West Indies and in Central and South America, was in the form of contracts which were little better than slavery. The swelling emigration to the Pacific coast of the United States, at first welcomed in that region as a supply of needed cheap labour, led to growing hostility among the white population, notably in California. The United States Government, in part with the consent of the Chinese Government, suspended the admission of Chinese labourers. In 1900, by unilateral action, the United States entirely prohibited it.

In the nearly three and a half decades from the close of the second war with Great Britain in 1860 to the outbreak of war with Japan in 1894, while not as acute as immediately before and after these years, the pressure from foreign governments continued to mount. The British treaty of 1858 provided that either China or the United Kingdom might ask for a revision after ten years. Although there was much discussion of proposed changes, the chief ones were made in 1876 by the Chefoo Convention. The British authorities were able to obtain it because of the murder near the border between China and Burma of Margary, of the British consular service. The Chefoo Convention obtained not only an indemnity for Margary's death but also some other concessions, among them the opening of more ports for trade.

Here and there Western powers were nibbling at the borders of China. In 1863 France made Cambodia a protectorate. In the 1860's she annexed Cochin-China, previously a province of Annam. In 1874 she obtained extra-territorial privileges in Annam for all Europeans and the opening of more ports for commerce and of the Red River to foreign navigation. In 1883 and 1884 she extended her protectorate over all of Annam. The Chinese were disturbed, for, while not an integral part of the Empire and in the European sense not exactly a protectorate, Annam was a dependency of Peking in a fashion peculiar to Chinese practice. As a result fighting began between the French and the Chinese, but it was somewhat desultory, and in 1885 peace was patched up by the recognition by Peking of the French protectorate in Annam and freedom of trade between Tongking, the northernmost section of Annam, and the adjacent Chinese provinces. Beginning early in the nineteenth century, the English had been advancing in Burma, which was also in a tributary relationship to China. In 1886 they completed their conquest of the country. That same year China consented, but with the provision that the decennial tribute-bearing mission from Burma should continue to be sent to Peking. In 1887 China formally ceded Macao to Portugal, thus acknowledging what had long been an actuality. She did so, however, with the stipulation that the territory should never be alienated to a third power without her consent.

In the 1870s Russia made an ominous advance in the far west. Chinese rule sat rather uneasily on the western fringes of Sinkiang, where the Manchus had extended the Empire only slightly over a century before and where Chinese were a very small minority. One of the rebellions which threatened Manchu rule in the 1860s brought unrest and seemed to be about to tear away much of Sinkiang, especially in portions which adjoined the Russian Empire. In 1871 Russia moved troops across the border into Ili. She sought to allay Chinese fears by promising to remove them when Peking was in a position to maintain order in the region. When Tso Tsung-t'ang had subdued the revolt, China asked Russia to fulfil that promise, but in the ensuing prolonged negotiations the latter obtained (1879) the cession of a portion of Ili and extensive privileges in Sinkiang. When the terms of the treaty became public, indignation in Peking almost led to war. Calmer counsels prevailed and a special envoy to St Petersburg obtained a more favourable settlement.

Ominous were also the activities of the Japanese. As we have suggested, in the third quarter of the nineteenth century Japan moved out of her self-imposed isolation and adopted and adapted much from the Occident. Concurrently she began to expand her borders, and in doing so made advances into Chinese spheres of influence which were precursors of attempts in the next century to control all that empire. In 1875 she acquired full title to the Kurile

Islands, surrendering in return to Russia her claim to Sakhalin, and in 1878 she annexed the Bonin Islands. In neither of these moves did she threaten Chinese interests, but they were symptomatic of an expansionist policy which boded ill for her huge neighbour. Slightly earlier, also in the 1870s, Japan extended her rule to the Ryukyu Islands. Both Japanese and Chinese had claimed the islands, the former because they had been considered a part of the fief of one of their feudal lords, and the latter because they had long been paying 'tribute' to Peking. The Japanese forced a clear-cut settlement by demanding satisfaction from China for the murder of some Ryukuans who had been wrecked on the shores of Formosa. China demurred, denying both Japan's authority in the Ryukyus and her own responsibility for the Formosans. Japan countered by sending a punitive expedition to Formosa. Through the good offices of the British minister at Peking the controversy was settled by the payment by China to Japan of an indemnity. Japan retained possession of the Ryukyus.

More immediately serious was friction over Korea. That country, constituting a peninsula lying strategically between China, Japan, and Eastern Siberia, became a bone of contention among the first two powers and Russia. From time to time across the centuries both China and Japan had occupied part of it. Under the Ch'ing Dynasty, Korea sent annual 'tribute-bearing' embassies to Peking, thus acknowledging the kind of suzerainty peculiar to China's relations with several border states. In general it did not entail direction or supervision of the tributary's internal affairs. Until the 1870's Korea insisted on maintaining an aloofness from the Western powers who had forced themselves upon China and Japan. In 1876 Japan, taking action similar to that of these powers in the Far East, by a naval demonstration off the coast of Korea obtained from that country a treaty of amity and commerce in which she declared Korea to be 'an independent state' with 'the same sovereign rights' as herself. Whether intentionally or not, this challenged the Chinese claim to suzerainty. Partly on Chinese advice as a way of counteracting Japan, in the 1880's Korea concluded treaties with several Western governments, most of whom made their envoy in Peking also their representative in Korea. These actions precipitated anti-foreign riots in Seoul. Both China and Japan sent forces to restore order. China began to take a more active part in Korea's internal affairs. Clashes between Japanese and Chinese troops in Seoul followed. In April, 1885, China and Japan signed a convention by which they agreed to withdraw their troops within four months, each was to notify the other in case it again sent troops into Korea, and Korea was to be encouraged to organize her own modern army under the direction of one who was neither Chinese nor Japanese. For a time this official seemed about to be obtained from Russia, but under pressure from Great Britain, Japan, and China the Korean monarch was constrained to withdraw from the arrangement. For the moment Russian ambitions were scotched. Representing China in Korea was Yüan Shih-k'ai, whom we are to meet again in later stages of our story. Continued friction in Korea between Japan and China was inevitable and it was this, as we shall see in a moment, which precipitated the developments that swept aside China's historic culture.

Through the several channels which we have described the way was being prepared for the later revolution. The symptoms were only beginning to appear and Western visitors to China early in the 1890's saw the old order as adamant and unshaken. Leading Chinese and Manchus resisted change. For instance, it was only reluctantly and after much delay that the foreign envoys in Peking were received in audience by the Emperor. Even then it was by subtle face-saving arrangements which partially soothed the traditional Chinese conviction of the Empire's superiority over all other countries. Not until November 1894, after the first defeats in the war with Japan, was an audience held according to protocol which entirely satisfied the ministers of the Western world. Yet China was already making concessions. Some of these we have noted. Another, the full import of which was not yet perceived, was the increasing load put on the central government, a load which was contrary to the genius of Chinese political practice. Traditionally the Emperor had left much discretion to provincial authorities. In a realm as large as China and without the rapid means of communication of the nineteenth- and twentieth-century world, this was almost necessary. Under that precedent the earlier wars of the nineteenth century had been waged. Parts of the Empire were engaged while those portions which were distant from the scene of battle were scarcely aware of the hostilities. Peking held accountable the provincial authorities who were directly involved. Now the central government was more and more pressed, and at a time when it was in the hands of a decrepit dynasty. Foreign powers insisted on treating directly with Peking, on having resident legations in that city, and on audiences with the Emperor on the basis of full equality. Again and again in its unsuccessful resistance Peking was required to pay an indemnity, thus placing additional burdens on the imperial finances. The Imperial Maritime Customs Service was managed closely from Peking by Hart. The central government was having to take on more and more functions. Had there been far-seeing men of ability at the helm the adjustment might have been made. However, with minors on the throne and Tz'ŭ Hsi in control this could scarcely be expected. With incompetents in charge, the ancient political structure creaked and within less than twenty years after 1894 collapsed.

CHAPTER FIVE

THE OLD ORDER CRUMBLES: 1894–1912.

CONFLICT over Korea set off a series of shocks which, added to the accumulated pressures of the preceding decades, destroyed the chief bulwarks of the old order in China. Fatally weakened, that order crumbled. Revolution swept across the land. By the middle of the twentieth century, so far from having reached its term, it seemed only to be in mid-course and still to be moving from one stage to another. An early stage culminated in 1911 and 1912. By the first few weeks of the latter year two of the three chief foundation stones of Confucian society, the civil service examinations and the monarchy, had been removed, and a third, the traditional pattern of the schools, had been dealt such blows that it was rapidly disintegrating. The civilization which had been in process of construction since at least the second millennium before Christ, and under which lived the largest fairly homogeneous body of mankind, was collapsing. Fragments remained, but they too were threatened.

The first of the shocks came in the summer of 1894. Rivalry in Korea between China and Japan mounted, only temporarily eased by the convention of 1885. Korea was torn by factions. Its royal house was incompetent and its administration was weak. A dominant issue was whether the country should conform to the Occident. In the main those who wished no change looked to China for support and those who advocated reorganization admired Japan, as a land which was accomplishing it in its own borders with startling success. Chinese and Japanese agents added to the tensions. Early in 1894 a revolt flared up in Korea, led by the Tonghak, a secret society, which demanded the expulsion of all foreigners, especially the Japanese. At the request of the Korean monarch, probably inspired by Yüan Shih-k'ai, the Chinese sent in troops to help suppress the revolt and, as in duty bound by the agreement of 1885, notified Japan of their action, promising the withdrawal of the forces as soon as the uprising was suppressed. Japan also dispatched armed detachments. Before the arrival of aid from either China or Japan, the Korean Government had succeeded in putting down the Tonghak rebellion.

Japan now proposed that she and China undertake jointly the reorganization of the Korean regime. China declined, declaring that she did not customarily interfere in the internal affairs of a vassal state and that if, as Japan averred, Korea was independent neither power should do so. The Japanese thereupon announced their intention of taking unilateral action. They high-handedly obtained control of the Korean court and had it declare war on China and request the Japanese to expel the Chinese troops. The Japanese acted promptly and war followed.

The Chinese were quickly defeated on both land and sea. Some of their officers fought bravely, but others were incompetent. The Japanese forces moved into Chinese territory. They took Port Arthur, a strategic harbour on the Liaotung Peninsula which constituted a potential naval base commanding the sea approaches to Manchuria. They pursued the Chinese fleet to Weihaiwai, on the north shore of the Shantung promontory, opposite Manchuria, and forced the surrender of that stronghold together with such of the Chinese ships as remained afloat. The leading Chinese commanders committed suicide. The Japanese land forces crossed the Yalu into Manchuria and rapidly moved across it, threatening Peking from the north. However, before they penetrated south of the Great Wall peace negotiations were in full swing and were concluded before China proper was invaded.

The terms of the treaty were sufficiently galling to China. That document bore the name of Shimonoseki, from the place in Japan to which the Chinese negotiators were required to come. Japan might have insisted on even more sweeping conditions of peace had it not been for the attempted assassination by one of her subjects of the chief

Chinese representative, Li Hung-chang, and the desire of her government to make amends. By the treaty China recognized the full independence of Korea, thus renouncing her claims as suzerain which had provided her with an alleged reason for intervention in that land. She ceded to Japan the Liaotung Peninsula. That peninsula included the strategic harbour of Port Arthur and the city of Dairen (also known as Dalny and Talienwan), soon to become the chief port of entry to Manchuria. Japan thus acquired a position from which she commanded the sea approach both to the rich and undeveloped Manchuria and to Peking and the north of China proper. China ceded Formosa and the Pescadores Islands, with their predominantly Chinese population. With the exception of Sakhalin, if it can be called an exception, Japan now possessed the islands which curtained the east coast of Asia from immediately south of Kamchatka to the southern tip of Formosa. China opened four cities to Japanese subjects, including Chungking, in the remote interior on the upper Yangtze, and permitted Japanese steamers to ply on that river as far as that port. Under the most-favoured-nation clauses in the treaties with Western powers, these cities and that stretch of the Yangtze were likewise available to these countries. China also agreed to pay what for those days was a substantial indemnity.

The Treaty of Shimonoseki was highly significant. It marked an important early stage in Japan's advance against China, an advance which was to continue intermittently until it was decisively halted and thrown back during World War II. In addition it became the occasion for demands by European powers on China which threatened the early dismemberment of the Empire.

Even before the treaty was signed it was known to at least one of China's advisers that Japan would not be allowed to hold all her takings. The treaty was signed in April. The following month France, Germany, and Russia brought such pressure on Japan that a few months later she returned the Liaotung Peninsula to China, receiving in return an added indemnity. France and Russia joined in competing with the English and the Germans for the privilege of lending China the sums needed.

Soon the powers began carving out for themselves leaseholds and spheres of influence, reinforcing and extending their footholds through concessions for the building of railways. Since this was an era of empire building and since in the 1880's and 1890's much of Africa had been partitioned among the earth-hungry European governments, the prospect for China's continued independence and territorial integrity was grim.

Germany made the murder of a German Catholic missionary in Shantung the excuse for occupying Kiaochow, the best harbour in that province, and in March 1898 obtained from China a ninety-nine year lease on it. She developed Tsingtao, the port on the bay, into a modern city. She demanded and was given permission to construct railways from it into the hinterland and to develop mines in the province. Russia had wished to acquire Kiaochow, but instead was granted footholds in Manchuria. It was continuous with the territory which she had annexed from China in the 1850's.

The very month in which the lease to Germany was signed Russia obtained one, to run for twenty-five years, to the southern tip of the Liaotung Peninsula, including Port Arthur and Dairen. Earlier, in 1896, China had agreed to permit Russia, who was then constructing a railway across Siberia, to build a connecting line directly across the northern part of Manchuria, a more direct route to the Pacific than the one in Russian territory along the Amur and Ussuri Rivers. China also agreed to seek through Russian banks the funds needed for railways north of the Great Wall, a system which came to be known as the Chinese Eastern Railway. Russia ear-marked for herself all of Chinese territory contiguous with her own, a policy which in a less obvious guise was to be continued under the Communist regime which late in 1917 became heir of that of the Tsars.

France extended northward into China the tentacles of

her growing empire in Indochina. In April 1898 she acquired a ninety-nine-year lease on the Bay of Kwangchow, in Kwangtung Province, and demanded and obtained the assurance that China would not alienate to a third power all or part of the provinces bordering on Tongking. Over the course of four years, from 1896 into 1899, France also sought and was given concessions for building railways in these provinces. Of these the most important was one which issued in a narrow gauge line from Tongking to Yünnanfu, also known as Kunming, which was to become a significant means of access to West China during the Japanese invasion in the 1930s and 1940s.

In April 1898 Japan, significantly, asked China not to alienate to another power any territory in Fukien, opposite her recently acquired Formosa. China replied that she would not grant any portion of that province to any power, thus making it clear that she did not propose to allow Japan to make it a sphere of influence.

In 1898, with French and Russian support, the Belgians obtained a contract to provide funds through a loan to construct the strategic trunk railway from Peking to Hankow and attempted, although in this they were checkmated by the Chinese, to acquire control of the project to extend that line to Canton.

As the leader in China's foreign trade and in opening China to the outer world, Great Britain viewed with concern this threat of partition and the strong possibility that through it in much of the Empire barriers would be erected by her rivals against her merchants and bankers. Partly as a protection, especially against Russia, then regarded by her as her major enemy in Asia, Great Britain obtained (1898) a lease on Weihaiwei, almost opposite the Liaotung Peninsula, 'for as long a period as Port Arthur shall remain in the possession of Russia.' Also in 1898 she acquired a ninety-nine-year lease on land which extended the holdings in Kowloon, on the mainland opposite Hongkong, which had been ceded her in 1860. In February 1898 a few weeks before the spate of leases set in, she was formally assured by

China that none of the provinces adjoining the Yangtze would be alienated to any other power. This seemed to ensure her continued access to the markets of the heart of China proper. Great Britain also sought to stake out the Yangtze Valley as a preserve for railway development by her capital. This she did partly by concessions from China and partly by agreements with Germany and Russia for reciprocal respect as to railway building in their spheres of influence. In these fateful years of scramble for portions of China some other railway concessions were marked out, but none as weighted with possibilities of partition as were these.

The United States made but little effort to share in the prospective spoils of the seemingly moribund China. To be sure, there were Americans who attempted to obtain some of the concessions for building railways, but this came to nothing in actual construction. However, there was no lack of interest on the part of the United States. The westward drive which had carried that country across North America to the Pacific had as part of its dream the development of what was regarded as the vast market of China. Moreover, in 1898, the very year in which the European powers were scrambling for leaseholds and spheres of influence, the United States annexed Hawaii and the Philippines. Thus she moved boldly out into the Pacific, as she had tentatively begun to do in Samoa two decades earlier, and established herself at the very threshold of China.

No small part of the lure, especially for the retention of the Philippines, was that will-o'-the-wisp which had long been a goal of the westward expansionists, the China market. If China were now to be partitioned the new possessors would almost certainly raise discriminatory barriers. President McKinley, in coming out for annexation of at least part of the Philippines after the defeat of Spain, said frankly that it was for the purpose of 'the enlargement of American trade' and declared his policy to be for the 'open door' in the Orient for Americans and for other nations as well.

This seems to have been the first use of that term in official documents of the United States. The term was to become the corner-stone of that nation's policy in the Far East, and especially in China. At least some of the British were not unwilling to have the United States enunciate the principle, for it would reinforce the traditional policy from which they were retreating only from the desire to conserve something for themselves in the event of the division of China.

Partly at the suggestion of a British subject who had served in the Imperial Maritime Customs Service and over the signature of John Hay, then Secretary of State, in September 1899 notes were sent to the major European powers and to Japan asking that they give formal assurance that within their respective spheres of influence they would not interfere with any treaty port or vested interest, that only the Chinese Government should collect duties, that these would be according to the Chinese treaty tariff, and that no preferential harbour dues or railway rates would be given their subjects. The notes also asked that the powers co-operate in obtaining this assurance from one another. Even this somewhat mild although explicit application of the open door met with cool and evasive responses. Yet the principle thus put forward was to have results of high importance and vast dimensions. Moreover, whether for this or other reasons, China was not partitioned.

Even before the United States had taken its first modest steps towards checking the threatened partition of the Empire numbers of Chinese were urging action by their people and their governments to avert that fate. Reform societies were organized. Sponsored by one of the outstanding viceroys, Chang Chih-tung, a series of essays under the imperative title *Learn* came out, urging that if China were to avoid the fate of other countries which had fallen victims to the Occident, some of the methods of the West must be adopted. The writings of a British missionary, Timothy Richard, with a similar objective, enjoyed a wide circulation.

There were Chinese who advocated even more drastic measures. Among them was Sun Yat-sen. The son of a humble peasant-farmer who lived not far from Canton, by the initiative and aid of an older brother who had made his home in Hawaii, at the age of thirteen Sun had gone to those islands, had three years in a school conducted by an Anglican bishop, and had become convinced of the truth of Christianity. Returning to his native village, he expressed his new faith by defacing the images in a local temple and because of that deed was forced to flee. He received further education at the hands of Westerners, most of them Protestant missionaries, in Canton and Hongkong, was baptized, and was given a medical diploma. However, he was more interested in changing China than in practising his profession. He plotted the overthrow of the dynasty, fled the country to escape arrest and execution, and, a wanderer among his fellow-countrymen overseas, sought to enlist their support in attaining that objective.

More influential at the time than Sun Yat-sen was a group of radicals whose most prominent member was K'ang Yu-wei. In contrast with Sun, K'ang's training was fully Chinese. Professing to find support in the teaching of Confucius and of the ancient classics revered by Confucian scholars, he formulated a social and political programme which included the erasure of national boundaries, the abandonment of the family, the rearing of children and the care of the aged in public institutions, and the election of officials by popular franchise. As immediate steps he proposed less radical measures.

In the summer and early autumn of that fateful year, 1898, when the granting of leaseholds and the delimiting of spheres of influence seemed to portend the partition of China, K'ang Yu-wei and some others of like mind won the ear and the support of the young Emperor, him whom we usually know by his reign title, Kuang Hsü. Intelligent and studious, the Kuang Hsü Emperor wished to save his realm. During 'the hundred days of reform', in his name decrees were issued which at the moment appeared to be sweeping but which from the standpoint of later years were moderate. They included the reorganization of the army and navy, the end of useless sinecures, a new system of schools in which both the old and the Occidental learning would be taught, and changes in the civil service examinations. Reared in the palace and not a man of great physical or moral force, the Emperor lacked the skill, the experience, and the strength of character to carry through what he had begun.

The old order was not to be easily unseated and protests against the measures were vigorous and vocal. Tz'ŭ Hsi had been closely watching developments. In September 1898, angered by his attempt to kill Jung-lu, one of her closest and oldest friends, as a step towards checkmating her, the masterful Empress Dowager seized control, constrained the luckless Kuang Hsü Emperor to request her to resume the reins of government, had him confined to a section of the palace, and more or less subtly subjected him to continued humiliation, much of it public. She would quite possibly have found a way of having him die had it not been for the pointed solicitude of prominent Chinese and the foreign legations. Those who had served him as advisers were either executed or escaped by going abroad. Among the latter was K'ang Yu-wei. Most of the reforming decrees were annulled.

Reaction became more violent and culminated in a blind effort of some of the masses, which obtained the support of a few of the officials, to sweep out of the country the foreigner and all his hated ways. It was chiefly in the north and was spear-headed by units of the militia which were known as the I Ho T'uan or I Ho Ch'üan. From the latter, which may be translated as 'Righteous Harmony Fists', and from their physical exercises they were called by foreigners 'the Boxers'. They had such slogans as 'Protect the country, destroy the foreigner', and 'Protect the Ch'ing [dynasty], destroy the foreigner'. With the militia were associated members of some of the secret societies which abounded in China and rowdy elements which rejoiced in the opportunity for violence and plunder. In accordance with traditions of long standing, the Boxers believed that magic could render them invulnerable. This they invoked against the foreigners' bullets.

As early as 1899 the Boxers were killing Chinese Christians as dupes and tools of the hated aliens. But it was in the summer of 1900 that the madness reached its peak. To protect members of their legations in Peking a body of troops of several nations attempted to make its way to the capital. Attacked, it was compelled to retreat to Tientsin. To protect the foreigners in that city a force representing six nations took by assault the forts which guarded the approach by river. The Empress Dowager and some of her advisers joined with the Boxers in interpreting this as an act of war. Tz'ŭ Hsi ordered that all foreigners in the realm be killed. Those in Peking and the immediate neighbourhood gathered in the legations, grouped as most of them were in a section next to the south wall of the city, and in a Catholic church and stood siege. The legation staff had considered complying with the instructions of the Chinese court to leave the city and accept a promised safe-conduct to the coast, but the shooting of the German minister by a Chinese soldier who declared that he was acting under orders decided them to remain in Peking. Relief came in the middle of August, when an expedition assembled by the powers fought its way through from Tientsin. The Old Buddha thereupon fled from the city, taking the Emperor with her, but not before, as an act of spite, she had had his favourite concubine thrown down a well. She and the court found haven in Hsian, where in centuries past had been the proud capital under the name of Ch'ang-an.

In the meantime the Boxers were attacking foreigners and Chinese Christians in other parts of the country. The destruction of life was especially severe in the north and northeast. In some places, notably in the province of Shansi, where there was a rabidly anti-foreign governor, officials gave support to the Boxers and even went beyond them. Several thousand Chinese Christians and several scores of missionaries lost their lives. A large proportion of the foreigners in the interior took refuge in the ports or left the country.

In suppressing the movement and rescuing and protecting their nationals, in some places foreign troops were as ruthless as the Boxers. Much of Peking was looted and thousands of its inhabitants either committed suicide or were slaughtered. Contingents of foreign troops raised the siege of beleaguered foreigners in other centres and as they did so took punitive measures.

Cooler heads among both Chinese and foreigners forestalled what must have been, but for their action, even worse destruction. The admirals commanding the foreign fleets off Tientsin declared it to be their purpose to use force only against the Boxers and those who opposed the expedition sent to raise the siege of the legations. The viceroys in the Yangtze Valley and the south made known their intention of obeying the treaties and protecting the lives and property of foreigners. At least two governors in the north took a similar attitude. On this occasion the traditional lack of tight centralized control and of a large degree of discretion on the part of provincial authorities proved an advantage. Most of China did not heed what amounted to a declaration of war by Peking on the Occident and Japan. Thus the loss of life was greatly reduced and an even more humiliating defeat was prevented.

The consequences for China of the Boxer outbreak were serious enough. Russia moved troops into Manchuria, ostensibly to protect her subjects and to restore order, but it was clear that continued control and even open or covert annexation were her goals. The United States Government, fearing that the partition of China threatened only a few months before might become an actuality, attempted to forestall it. On 3 July 1900, Secretary of State Hay sent a circular note to the powers declaring it to be the purpose of his government to 'act concurrently with the other powers' in restoring order and protecting the lives and property of its citizens, and 'to seek a solution which may bring about permanent safety and peace in China, preserve Chinese territorial and administrative entity, protect all rights guaranteed to friendly powers by treaty and international law, and safeguard for the world the principle of equal and impartial trade with all parts of the Chinese Empire.' He thus went further than in his notes of the previous September. Probably the note had little effect in moderating the demands of the powers. Like its predecessors it was of importance chiefly for the fashion in which the United States committed itself to a policy which in the decades ahead was to embroil it ever more deeply in Chinese affairs with major consequences both for itself and for China. Yet again, whether or not because of Hay's action, China escaped partition.

A settlement was eventually reached, in September 1901, in what was known as a protocol. It was signed by representatives of China, nine European powers, Japan, and the United States. Its more significant terms were the report by the Chinese Government of its punishment of the officials who had been chiefly responsible for the attacks on foreigners; the prohibition by China of arms and ammunition for two years, with the provision that it could be extended if the powers deemed it necessary; the payment by China of an indemnity of 450,000,000 taels, about £67,000,000, over a period of forty years, a sum which in those days seemed gigantic; the stationing of permanent foreign guards in the legation quarter in Peking as a means of protection against a possible renewal of the threat; for the same purpose the occupation by foreign forces of certain posts to ensure free communication between the legations and the sea; and the raising of the Office of Foreign Affairs (Tsungli Yamen) to a Ministry of Foreign Affairs (Wai-wu-pu), giving it precedence over all the other ministries of state, thus according relations with foreign powers a dignity which they had not hitherto possessed and once for all cancelling the subordinate status to which China had traditionally relegated foreign peoples and governments.

From now on for a quarter of a century and more Westerners in China behaved as though the Empire was a conquered occupied country. The attitude of most of them towards the Chinese was supercilious and even arrogant. It was clear that any violence against a Westerner would be met by prompt and vigorous reprisal. Foreign gunboats as well as commercial steamers plied the coastal waters and the

Yangtze and its tributaries. In Peking the legations resembled a fortress guarded by their own troops.

Here was galling defeat differing from anything which China had previously known. Conquest by foreigners was no new experience. Repeatedly, as we have seen, China had been invaded and part or all of it ruled by aliens. Indeed, the Manchus, then in power, had come in by this means. However, the conquest had always been by land and from the north or north-west, and by peoples of cultures which were palpably inferior to that of China. Now the invaders were from both land and sea and from the east and south-east as well as from the north and north-west. Moreover, they represented cultures which were more powerful and dynamic than that of China. Until now the Chinese had conserved their culture as against foreign conquerors, and some of the latter had conformed to it. Now they must conform to the culture of the invaders or lose their political independence.

As if to accentuate China's plight the Boxer outbreak led directly to a war between Russia and Japan which was fought chiefly on Chinese soil and in Chinese waters while China stood by, helpless. After the suppression of the Boxers and the conclusion of the Protocol of 1901, Russia kept her troops in Manchuria. Presumably she intended to remain there and possibly to annex the area. Her energies engaged in the Boer War, Britain was unable to contemplate armed measures to dislodge the Russians. Yet through much of the nineteenth century one of her major concerns had been the advance of Russia in the Balkans and in Asia. To obtain a friend in her effort to check Russia in China, in January 1902 she entered into an alliance with Japan, for that country also had cause to fear Russia. Secretary Hay had sought by representations to St Petersburg to preserve the open door in Manchuria, but to no avail. In October 1903 he negotiated a commercial treaty with China whereby the latter agreed to open to foreign residence and trade two additional cities in Manchuria, thus seeking to keep that region from becoming a Russian preserve. It was left to Japan to take active measures effectively to check Russia. She was alarmed by the Russian advance and especially Russian ambitions in Korea. These threatened the interests in that country for which she had recently fought China. Negotiations failed to win from Russia what seemed to the Japanese satisfactory assurances. Thereupon (February 1904) Japan suddenly struck. China declared her neutrality, but this did not prevent pitched battles on her soil in Manchuria. There were fears that neutral powers might take advantage of the situation to partition China. To try to forestall this action, Hay, still Secretary of State of the United States, asked and received assurances from Great Britain, France, Germany, and Italy that they would not demand compensation in any form for services rendered to the belligerents.

By the Treaty of Portsmouth (September 1905), which ended the Russo-Japanese War, Japan obtained the Russian rights in the Liaotung Peninsula, thus in part regaining that of which Russia, France, and Germany had deprived her ten years before. She was also given the Russian share in the railways of South Manchuria. Although both Russia and Japan promised to withdraw all their troops from Manchuria except such as might be needed to guard the railways and declared that they would not stand in the way of measures which China might take to develop the resources of Manchuria in such fashion that all countries would have equal access to them, and although they said that the Manchurian railways would be used for purely commercial and not political purposes, and in spite of the fact that Russia formally declared that she did not have in Manchuria 'any territorial advantages or preferential or exclusive concessions in impairment of Chinese sovereignty or inconsistent with the principle of equal opportunity', both Russia and Japan were firmly planted in that land of potential untapped wealth. Japan especially felt herself entitled to special privileges in return for her expenditure of life and treasure. In connexion with the treaty which China entered into with Japan assenting to such provisions of the Treaty of

Portsmouth as dealt with her interests, she signed a secret agreement which gave to Japan additional privileges in Manchuria.

The chief opponent of special concessions in Manchuria was the United States. In the summer of 1905 an American railway magnate, E. H. Harriman, negotiated with the Japanese an agreement whereby he was to provide the capital for the rebuilding of the South Manchurian Railway, but this was not carried out. In June 1906 the vivid, ambitious, and youthful Willard Straight was appointed Consul-General for the United States in Mukden. He had been in Korea and his anger had been aroused by the progressive Japanese absorption of that country and what he regarded as the supine acquiescence of his government in it (Japan made Korea a protectorate in 1905 and formally annexed it in 1910). He now dreamed of countering Japan in Manchuria. He would do this by the development of American trade and investment in that region. As Acting Chief of the Far Eastern Division of the Department of State from November 1908 to June 1909, he encouraged Harriman in a project, which proved abortive because of Harriman's death, for the purchase of the Russian interest in the Chinese Eastern Railway as a step in a globe-encircling railway empire. Late in 1909 Knox, American Secretary of State, proposed to Great Britain, Russia, and Japan the neutralization of the Manchurian railways and co-operation in building one of the proposed lines in that area. The three powers rejected the plan. Indeed, it proved an incentive towards driving the Japanese and the Russians together in a treaty (July 1910) in which the two agreed to respect each other's rights in Manchuria and to consult with each other if they were threatened. Great Britain welcomed the accord as promoting understanding and friendship between two countries, recently at war with each other, whose support she now needed in her rising competition with Germany.

How would the Chinese meet this series of blows? Even though technically the Boxer madness had not embroiled them in war with the powers, actually they had been defeated in a more humiliating fashion than in any of their conflicts of the nineteenth century. A formal declaration of war by the powers and the acceptance of the status of belligerents by the great viceroys of the Yangtze Valley and the south might have issued in more abject prostration, and perhaps in the partition of the Empire. Yet even without it, as we have said, China entered the twentieth century in a virtual state of foreign occupation. Ostensibly she was still a sovereign state, but her independence had been compromised, first by the treaties of the nineteenth century, and now by the outcome of the Boxer outbreak and the Russo-Japanese War and its aftermath. Here, as we have pointed out in the Preface, was a conflict of cultures. Of a kind which was without precedent in China's long history, it could not be met in the traditional fashion enjoined by Confucian principles. How was the conflict to be resolved? Was it to be by holding the Westerner at arm's length or by his forcible expulsion? The first had been tried in the nineteenth century, and the second in the Boxer year, and had resulted in the near enslavement of China. It was now obvious that these meant ruin. Was the conflict to be superseded by the complete erasure of the old and the substitution of importations from the West? Few if any were as yet prepared to advocate or accept this possibility. That effort was to wait until mid-century and the Communists. Could there be worked out an integration of the old and the new, one which would incorporate the best features from the inherited culture with what could be learned from the Occident? If so, what form or forms would that integration take? Would it issue in a hodge-podge of the two, a caricature of both, or would there be such fresh creativity that a culture would emerge which, while incorporating much from China's past and from the West, would be distinctive and make significant and important contributions to mankind?

The prospect was not encouraging. The state was headed by a decadent foreign dynasty, with an intelligent but weak Emperor and having as its dominant personality Tz'ŭ Hsi, forceful, astute in so manipulating the court and individuals in it as to get her own way, but superstitious, utterly selfish, and blind to the full significance of the forces that were impinging on the Empire. The able Chinese leadership which had rescued the dynasty from the doldrums of the mid nineteenth century had either been removed by death or was elderly and soon to be gathered to its fathers. Tsêng Kuo-fan, who had been chiefly responsible for suppressing the T'ai P'ing revolt and who had been far-sighted enough to see that some accommodation must be made to the West, had been gone since 1872. His fellow-provincial, Tso Tsung-t'ang, who had put down the rebellion which threatened to tear Sinkiang from the Empire, had died in 1885. Li Hung-chang followed him in November 1901, only a few weeks after the signing of the Boxer settlement. Chang Chih-tung lived on until 1909, but his main contribution had been made earlier, and in his later years he attempted to stem the tide towards change. These men, the product of the traditional Confucian education and the system of civil service examinations, had no successors of like stature. It is doubtful, indeed, whether that kind of training could produce men who were equal to the new day. It was a system which looked backward to idealized sage-monarchs and teachers and resented change. For several centuries it had been progressively less creative and content to search out and elaborate what had come down from the past. It had done much to conserve and perpetuate Chinese culture and had given China its remarkable unity and continuity, but it was not prepared to go to school to another civilization. Nor were the Manchu nobility and officials any better.

In this, as we have suggested, China was in striking contrast with Japan. At the risk of a wearying repetition we may again remind ourselves that the Japanese had long been eager to learn from other nations but at the same time to preserve their independence, and so to adapt what they took over from abroad as to reinforce what they inherited from their ancestors. For centuries they adopted much from China, so much so that in many of its aspects their culture appeared to be merely a variant of Chinese civilization. Yet they did so in such fashion as to emphasize their military tradition and the place of the imperial family. Nor did they allow the Buddhism which came to them by way of China to supplant the native religion, Shinto. For a time in the sixteenth century they were eager to learn from the Occident. However, when their political unity and independence seemed to them to be threatened, they resolutely kept the Occident at arm's length. In the mid nineteenth century some of the far-seeing among their youth saw that this was no longer possible and induced the nation to become a pupil of the West. Yet in doing so, as we have seen, such Japanese traditions were strengthened as the position of the Emperor, Shinto, and, to the later grief of the country, the place of the military. Even after the overwhelming defeat in World War II and occupation by the victors, Japan not only willingly learned from her conquerors but also held together and preserved her political independence and the core of her inherited culture.

This the Chinese proved unable to do. They threw over much of what was essential in their own culture. At first they sought to substitute the patterns and outlook of science, liberalism, and democracy seen in the United States and Great Britain. Then, owing in large part to an invasion from Japan which dealt disastrous blows to the government which was arising under that influence, in the mid-century China was captured by an enthusiastic and ruthless Communism which sought to erase all in the nation's past which it deemed inconsistent with its purpose, looking to Russia for its inspiration and patterns. It is that story, here so briefly summarized, whose main outlines we are to trace in the ensuing pages.

First, and they properly belong in this chapter, we must tell of the attempts to preserve both the dynasty and the Confucian monarchy, integrating with them the main contributions from the West, and in such fashion as to restore the independence which had been compromised in the preceding half century and more.

The lesson of 1900 and 1901, with its evidence of the overwhelming power of the Westerner, was not entirely lost on Tz'ŭ Hsi and her entourage. Much as they might dislike it, she and some of the others were convinced that if the dynasty was to be preserved changes must come and at least an outward face of friendliness must be presented to the foreigner. Even before she left Hsian, Tz'ŭ Hsi had an edict issued in the name of the Emperor which ordered innovations. Once more in Peking, she made a point of giving formal audience to the representatives of the powers and of again and again receiving affably the women of the foreign community. In some ways she attempted to restore the past. She had repaired and rebuilt some of the structures at her favourite resort, the Summer Palace, which had been damaged or destroyed by the invading troops. She took steps for the permanence of Manchu rule. A majority of the highest posts in the central bureaucracy in Peking were still filled with Manchus rather than Chinese. Yet an important departure from tradition was permission for intermarriage between Chinese and Manchus. Moreover, steps were taken towards adjusting China to the Occident which a decade earlier would have seemed breath-taking. Manchu youth were encouraged to study abroad at the expense of the government. Yüan Shih-kai, who had earned the Empress Dowager's gratitude by betraying the confidence of the Emperor in 1898, when he had ordered Yüan to seize and execute Jung-lu as a preliminary to action against her own person, was made viceroy of the province of Chihli, in which Peking was situated, and was ordered to reorganize the army after Occidental patterns.

More drastic was an act of 1905. The ancient system of competitive civil service examinations was abolished and instead graduation from one of the new schools modelled on those of the West was to be the road to office. Thus was removed what in some respects was the corner-stone of the edifice of traditional Chinese culture. As we have seen, these examinations had been begun at least as far back as the Han Dynasty. Across the centuries they had been elaborated. Through them the most coveted honours of the Empire were to be obtained. Those who passed successfully through the gruelling tests and attained the highest degrees were renowned throughout the realm, and through them appointment to the highest posts was possible. The examinations were based upon the writings revered by Confucian scholars. China's schools were designed to prepare students to compete in them. The end of the civil service examinations meant that this kind of school died out. It did not disappear immediately. However, the new schools which purveyed Western knowledge rapidly supplanted it. In the curricula of many of these schools the Confucian classics were given a place, but as a rule they were poorly taught; students were interested chiefly in the subjects which had a market value, mainly the natural and social sciences and engineering, and if they studied the ancient books it was usually only from compulsion and half-heartedly. This meant that for members of the younger generation Confucianism was a declining force. They were usually intensely patriotic, and the infection of nationalism from the West combined with a traditional pride in Chinese culture and an inherited sense of the importance of the scholar to make the new student class eager and often turbulent agitators in political and international issues. Yet the Confucianism which had shaped their predecessors became a fading memory.

In 1906 an imperial decree dealt with what had become a major curse, the smoking of opium. It ordered the progressive elimination of the growth of the opium poppy in China and of the use of the drug by those under sixty years of age and the prohibition of its use by government employees. The British, the chief importers of the drug, agreed to reduce the amount brought in by one-tenth a year. Before long (1912) an international convention broadened the efforts at suppression. As a result, for several years progress was achieved in ridding the realm of the debilitating habit, but the gains were to be largely nullified in the years of internal political disorder which followed the end of the dynasty.

Imperial edicts also undertook the gradual introduction of constitutional government on the pattern of that found in liberal regimes in the West. In the autumn of 1905 a commission appointed by imperial decree began a tour of the Occident to study administration with a view to advising on reforms. In September 1906, after the return of the commission, another decree promised, within the framework of the monarchy, constitutional government based upon popular suffrage, a revision of the laws, universal education, the regulation of finances, and the reorganization of the army. A few weeks later, in November 1906, the remodelling of the administration of the central government was ordered and a deliberative assembly with advisory functions was promised as a preparatory step towards a parliament. In 1907 a decree ordered the creation of provincial assemblies. Like the national assembly they were to be purely consultative bodies without power to enact legislation. Under pressure from those who believed that a time schedule should be set up, in August 1908 a decree gave the outline of a proposed constitution. In it the authority of the throne and the perpetuation of the dynasty were affirmed, a parliament was promised, a reshaping of the administrative structure was outlined, and provision was made for the progressive preparation of the country for participation in the proposed regime. The year 1917 was set as the time for the proclammation of the new form of government and the calling of the first parliament.

Whether, had the dynasty possessed strong leadership, the proposed reorganization would have been carried through and the monarchy preserved we cannot know. Whether, had she lived, Tz'ŭ Hsi could have accomplished it is another unanswerable question. As it was, on 14 November 1908, the Kuang Hsü Emperor died. The following day Tz'ŭ Hsi followed him. The near coincidence gave rise to rumours and speculation of foul play. It has been said that the unhappy Emperor had been murdered and that even the date of his death had been falsified. However, none of this has been confirmed. Shortly before her death Tz'ŭ Hsi named as the next Emperor an infant, P'u-i, less than three years of age and a nephew of his predecessor. Through his mother he was a grandson of Jung-lu. Jung-lu had died in 1903, and it is said that Tz'ŭ Hsi, loyal to his lifelong friendship, had promised him to put one of his descendants on the throne. The new reign was given the title Hsüan T'ung. The regent was the father of P'u-i and brother of the late Emperor. With him was to serve the widow of the late Emperor. Neither of these had the ability or force of character to guide the Empire and the dynasty through the stormy waters ahead. Nor was there among the Manchus in high places the needed wisdom. The strongest Chinese, Yüan Shih-kai, was in disfavour because of what was regarded as his betrayal of the regent's brother, the Kuang Hsü Emperor, which had precipitated the *coup d'état* of 1898 and had led to that ruler's virtual incarceration. Yüan was dismissed and allowed to retire to his estates in Honan, ostensibly because of an affection of his foot. There were not wanting those among foreign observers who expected the dynasty to be unseated or even to melt away and disappear at almost any moment.

In the meantime the tide of change was moving forward which was soon to sweep into desuetude the dynasty, and with it much of the old order. Schools incorporating Western subjects and methods were multiplying. It was reported that, as against 4,222 schools of a modern type with 102,767 pupils in 1905, in 1911 there were 52,650 schools of that kind with 1,625,534 students. Many, perhaps most, of these schools were inferior to their Western prototypes, for teachers trained in the new methods and the proper textbooks, libraries, and laboratories could not be acquired overnight. Schools conducted by Christian missionaries, especially by British and American Protestants, and of secondary and higher grades, grew in enrolments, staffs, and equipment. Translations of Western books were being made and published in large quantities. English was widely studied and was becoming the second language, subordinate only to Chinese.

Thousands of students went abroad to drink of the new learning. The majority went to Japan, for, as we have seen, for a generation that country had been developing schools which incorporated Occidental subjects and methods and the cost of travel, tuition, and living was much lower than in the Occident. Thanks, too, to the adoption by the Japanese centuries earlier of the Chinese written characters, the language difficulty was not as great as in Europe or America. Moreover, after 1905 Japan proved especially attractive, for it had demonstrated that by utilizing the appliances of the West an Asiatic power could defeat one of the hitherto seemingly invincible Occidental nations. Of those who went to the Occident more were in the United States than in either the British Isles or the Continent of Europe. The influx to the United States was increased by the remission of a substantial portion of the Boxer indemnity due to that government and the designation of those funds by China for the education of students going to that country. Since that remission was not made until 1908, the full effect did not begin to be seen until the next decade.

Nationalistic feeling began to make itself felt. In a sense it was a continuation of the traditional pride of culture. However, it was being reinforced by contact with the nationalism of the Occident and was aroused to fresh consciousness by the encroachments of foreign powers. In 1905 it found expression in a boycott of American trade in protest against the restrictions placed by the government of the United States on the immigration of Chinese.

Economic changes were in progress. Antimony, iron, and coal mines were being opened. Factories were springing up, notably for the manufacture of matches and cotton goods. Railways were being built, not only in Manchuria but also in China proper. By the end of 1908 it was possible to travel by rail from Western Europe to Hankow, in the very heart of the country, and a line was under construction to connect Hankow with Canton. Stock companies modelled on those of the West were appearing.

From Chinese who had taken refuge abroad came agitation for change, some of it anti-Manchu, and some through the printed page and some through organization. Thus

Liang Ch'i-ch'ao, of a scholarly family, who had competed successfully at an early age in the civil service examinations, and who had been a follower and pupil of K'ang Yu-wei and had fled from China to Japan when, in 1898, the Empress Dowager had put a sudden end to the reform movement, had a prolific and facile pen. Except for a tour in America and Australia, he spent the next twelve years or more in Japan. There he edited periodicals and wrote pamphlets in which he advocated reform. They had a wide circulation, especially among students. Master of the traditional literary style which appealed to those who had been reared to value it, no other single writer of the first decade of the twentieth century had as great an influence in bringing in the changes of the second decade. Yet he wished no quick sweeping aside of the past. He advocated, rather, an orderly even though rapid transition.

More drastic in his programme was Sun Yat-sen, whom we have already met. As we have suggested, he travelled widely among overseas Chinese in the United States, Britain, the Continent of Europe, and especially Asia. Much of his time he spent in Japan. To the Manchus he was a marked man and he lived under the shadow of a price which they placed on his head. He was not a scholar in the older Chinese sense of that term: he was not expert in the Confucian classics or the literary style which won rewards in the civil service examinations. He prided himself on his humble origin. Yet he read widely, especially in the political, social, and economic thought of the West. He had more than a nodding acquaintance with the writings of Henry George and Karl Marx. In his travels he stimulated the foundation of units of a revolutionary organization, the Hsing Chung Hui ('Prosper China Society'). In 1905 he organized in Tokyo, in part among the Chinese students who thronged that city, a revolutionary society, the T'ung Meng Hui. In contrast with the Hsing Chung Hui, which stood for moderate reform, it advocated the overthrow of the Manchus, the recovery of China for the Chinese, the establishment of a republic, the nationalization of the land, and world peace.

Sun Yat-sen was its president and Huang Hsing, who had led a revolt in the province of Hunan, was its vice-president. Groups to prepare the way for revolution sprang up in various parts of the Empire, chiefly in the Yangtze Valley and the south. Some of these were fostered by the T'ung Meng Hui or looked to it for moral support.

As a Protestant Christian Sun Yat-sen had a special welcome from Chinese of that faith. Among these friends was one who was baptized as Charles Jones Soong. Soong had come to the United States as a boy, had been befriended by Americans, had been given a Western education, much of it theological, and had returned to China as a Methodist missionary. There he married a wife of old Christian stock, after a time went into business in Shanghai, prospered, reared his children as Christians, and had them educated in the United States. As early as the mid-1890s he aided Sun Yat-sen financially. Later, but not until after 1912, one of his daughters became a secretary to Sun Yat-sen, and the latter married her although his first wife, also a Christian and the one who bore him his children, was still living. Three Soong daughters and the Soong son were to rise to prominence in the coming years, and in later stages in our story we are to meet them again.

Through a variety of additional ways the West was penetrating China. Outwardly in 1910 and the fore part of 1911, with the exception of the passing of the civil service examinations and the beginning of the changes in education and the government, the traditional structure of Chinese civilization was substantially intact. However, the Occident was pressing in, both directly and through the version of its culture which was represented by Japan. Christian missionaries, Roman Catholic, Protestant, and, to a less extent, Russian Orthodox, were continuing their penetration of the country. The severe reverse of the Boxer year proved only temporary. While in 1911 Christians numbered only about one in 200 of the population, this was twice their strength a decade earlier and they were to be found in every province of China proper and in Manchuria. Having had a prior start by more than two centuries, Roman Catholics still out-distanced the Protestants, but proportionately the latter were over-taking them. Missionary staffs had also increased, for churches in the British Isles, the continent of Europe, and North America saw in the crumbling of the barriers an opportunity and a challenge. Commerce was mounting. In the six years from 1898 to 1904, in spite of the Boxer inter-ruption, the monetary value of China's foreign trade in-creased by about half. In it British leadership was main-tained, but it was being threatened by the rapid growth of German trade and by the Japanese. Japanese steamers were beginning to be serious competitors to British steamers on the waters of the Yangtze and its tributaries. Foreign finan-cial interests were still looking to China as a field for the in-vestment of capital and continued to regard railways as enticing. A consortium of British, French, and German bankers negotiated a loan for the development of railways in Central China. The United States insisted that American bankers be admitted, and in May 1911 it was successful and the three-power loan became a four-power combination. It was this loan which helped to precipitate the revolution which ended Manchu rule, and with it the Confucian monarchy.

After the death of Tz'ŭ Hsi removed the last strong per-sonality in the dynasty, events, as we have suggested, hurried to a crisis. The Ch'ing Dynasty was obviously nearing its end. What would follow was by no means as clear. Had it not been for the complications introduced by the coming of the West, presumably events would have conformed to the traditional pattern. As we have reminded ourselves more than once, that pattern was fairly uniform. To understand what followed when it was discarded we must again sum-marize it. As a dynasty became weak and misfortunes over-took the Empire, the conviction spread through what might be called public opinion that the ruling family was losing the mandate of Heaven. The misfortunes might be natural, such as floods or drought. They might be man-made and palpably due to corrupt or inefficient administration. They might be rendered more acute by the increase of population during the earlier days of peace and good rule when the dynasty was in the first flush of vigour under the able men who founded it. The land would now not be able to bear the burden of the added number of mouths to be fed. Unrest would mount. Ambitious men would take advantage of it and rise in revolt, each seeking to supplant the reigning line and found a new one. A period of turmoil and civil strife, sometimes brief, sometimes prolonged, would follow. Occasionally a dynasty would display unexpected strength and achieve a new lease of life. That had happened, it will be recalled, to the Han in mid-course and to the T'ang a century and a half before its demise. As we have seen, the Ch'ing had been granted a reprieve in the third quarter of the nineteenth century. But sooner or later one of the contenders would fight his way to victory over his rivals, including the existing dynasty, place himself on the throne, and give so strong an administration that his family would be continued on it for several generations. The new dynasty would modify and add to what it inherited from its predecessor, but not since the third and second centuries before Christ, when the Han supplanted the shortlived and revolutionary Ch'in, had basic or drastic changes been made. Even before the first decade of the twentieth century the weakness of the Ch'ing was for all to see. Population had mounted, misgovernment and weakness were rife, and incompetent and selfish luxury had become general among the once sturdy and conquering Manchus. Again and again the Empire had been defeated in foreign wars. Its partition and loss of independence were prevented, not by the strength of the dynasty or the skill of its diplomacy, but by the jealousies and rivalries among the powers.

However, the coming of the West made impossible the repetition of the traditional pattern. New ideas had entered. Sun Yat-sen and others were demanding not only the ousting of the Manchus but also the substitution of a republic for the monarchy. These were being urged in a variety of ways Moderate voices that wished the retention of the monarchy insisted that the promised conformation to the constitutional patterns of the Occident be carried through and thus would make impossible the traditional persistence of the inherited institutions, even should the Manchus be followed by another dynasty. Moreover, foreign powers were to be reckoned with.

When death had removed Tz'ŭ Hsi the Ch'ing Dynasty quicky staggered to its fall, but not in the fashion of its predecessors. In October 1909 the provincial assemblies which had been projected in 1907 met for the first time. It was symbolic of the change that in one province which had been a centre of conservatism the structure which housed the assembly was a flimsy affair in Western style erected on the plot where once had stood the row after row of booths in which the civil service examinations had been given: the new, still only partly understood and with no assurance of permanence, was rising where once the old order had had a stronghold. These assemblies demanded that the national parliament should convene within two years and not in the proposed 1917. While this request was denied, when the first national assembly gathered in Peking in October 1910 and asked that the summoning of parliament be expedited, the regent so far yielded that the date was set forward to 1913. This concession did not satisfy the impatient assembly. The latter insisted that parliament be called immediately and that, after the manner of similar bodies in the Occident, the grand council, like the cabinets of some Western constitutional monarchies, be made responsible to it.

Unrest against the existing regime was augmented by actions arising in connexion with foreign loans. The national government at Peking became persuaded that railway construction by provincial interests was proving too slow and inefficient, and that the country would be better served if all the lines were constructed and managed on a comprehensive co-ordinated basis. It therefore decided to nationalize the railroads and to begin with the projects radiating from Chengtu, in the province of Szechwan, and with the projected line, on which work had been begun by pro-

vincial concerns, to connect Wuchang, on the south bank
of the Yangtze opposite Hankow, with Canton. Peking proposed to use for the latter purpose the proceeds of the loan
from the four-power consortium made in the spring of 1911.
Local opposition quickly developed. It was partly from the
traditional provincial particularism and against the extension of power by the central government. It was also because the local men of means who had invested in the railways feared that they would lose what they had put in.
Revolutionary groups who wished to overthrow the dynasty
took advantage of the situation. They plotted uprisings. One
in Canton was promptly crushed. One occurred in Szechwan. The strategic outbreak was in Wuchang, the capital
of the province of Hupeh. With its two sister cities Hankow
and Hanyang it constituted Wuhan, the main urban concentration at the heart of China proper and the key to the
centre of the Yangtze Valley.

The revolt in Wuchang was on the evening of 10 October 1911, called 'the double tenth', which the ensuing republic celebrated as its natal day. It took the form of an
attack by a body of government troops on the viceroy's
yamen, or offices. The viceroy incontinently fled. The rebels
persuaded a colonel, Li Yüan-hung, to head them. They
gave him, at first unwilling, the alternative of death and he
yielded and took command. They published a proclamation
in which they declared it their purpose to overthrow the
Manchus and to 'revive the rights of the Han People',
namely, the Chinese. They also expressed it as their purpose
to protect foreigners and Christian churches, thus seeking to
avoid possible intervention by the powers. Within four days
Wuchang, Hanyang, and Hankow were fully in the hands
of what called itself the People's Army. Before long the
People's Army came out flatly for a republic.

For a time the outcome seemed in doubt. To be sure,
within a month after 'the double tenth' most of the south
had cast in its lot with the revolutionaries, some centres in
the north had taken a similar stand, and several cities and
provinces had declared themselves neutral. The key port,

Shanghai, went over to the revolution and in it a provisional republican regime was set up. In a number of cities Manchus were massacred. In them the latter were theoretically garrisons to ensure the perpetuation of the conquest which had been effected in the seventeenth century. In the course of time they had become worthless from the military standpoint, living in idleness on government funds. In most places no mercy was shown them and thousands of men, women, and children were slaughtered and their possessions looted. In a panic, the Manchus abjectly called to their assistance Yüan Shih-k'ai, whom they had so recently dismissed. He delayed, pleading the continuation of the ill-health which had been the ostensible cause of his dismissal. When he assented, as he did shortly, it was on his own terms. He commanded the best army in the Empire, trained largely under his direction. Even before Yüan returned, the army had moved against the centre of the revolt, in the 'three cities'. Hankow was taken from the revolutionaries, and before long Hanyang was regained from them. The Emperor's advisers also incontinently yielded to the demand for the immediate inauguration of a constitutional monarchy, approving the outline of a document which, while it declared that the imperial line should continue, provided for a bicameral parliament, a premier elected by parliament and responsible to it, and excluded members of the imperial house from that post and several other high offices of state. Yüan Shih-k'ai was named by the throne as the first premier and was instructed to put the new regime in operation. He assumed the task and, supported by his army, it looked as though he might be able to hold at least part of the country to the remodelled monarchy. The powers declined to give financial aid to either side. Early in December Nanking fell to the republican forces and the ancient southern capital came into their hands. A few days thereafter an armistice was signed. In it Li Yüan-hung acted for the southern, or republican, forces. A peace conference between the two sides was called to meet in Shanghai.

While the peace conference was negotiating, different factions among the revolutionists met in Nanking and adopted a constitution for a republic. On 24 December 1911, Sun Yat-sen, who had been abroad, reached Shanghai and five days later was elected, by almost unanimous vote, Provisional President. Li Yüan-hung, commander-in-chief of the republican armies, was elected Vice-President. On 1 January 1912, Sun arrived in Nanking and took oath to dethrone the Manchus, establish a government based upon the will of the people, and then to resign that the people of China might elect their President. As a symbol of their rejection of Manchu rule, the adherents of the republic cut off their queues, the form of wearing the hair imposed on the men by the Manchus. Their troops compelled others in the regions ruled by them to do likewise.

Further bloodshed appeared to have been prevented and the unity of the country seemed to have been assured when, early in February, the Empress Dowager (the regent had been forced into retirement a few weeks earlier) issued a decree declaring that the dynasty would abdicate under suitable guarantees and appointing Yüan Shih-k'ai to negotiate with the People's Army to arrange the details. Yüan complied. On 2 February 1912, the formal abdication took place. P'u-i was permitted to retain the title of Emperor and the use of the imperial palace in Peking, and was promised an ample pension. The tombs of the Ch'ing Emperors were to be protected and that of the Kuang Hsü Emperor completed by the nation, the Manchu nobility were to retain their titles and for at least a time the members of the Manchu forces, the so-called Bannermen, were to receive their accustomed support. Manchus were to be citizens of the republic on an equality with Chinese. The Republic of China was declared to be a union of five peoples – Chinese, Manchus, Mongols, Moslems, and Tibetans. Sun Yat-sen protested that the Ch'ing Dynasty did not have the right to found a republic or to determine the form of government for the country and insisted that this could be done only by the people of China. However, to ensure unity and domestic peace, he resigned the Provisional Presidency and induced the National Assembly in Nanking to elect Yüan Shih-k'ai in his stead. Yüan accepted. Thus China embarked upon what for her was an untried experiment with a republic.

Even more significant than the venture with a republic was the abandonment of the monarchical form of government. That government had been in existence from the dawn of China's history. Since the early days of the Han Dynasty, in the third century before the Christian era, in theory China had been governed by Confucian principles. Orthodox Confucian teaching held that, except for the brief interlude of the Ch'in Dynasty in that same century, Confucianism had been the basis of government from the days of Yao, Shun, and Yü. As we have seen, for at least 2,000 years Confucianism had constituted the foundation of Chinese culture, its most characteristic feature, and the chief tie holding it together. Confucian principles were the major factor in determining standards of conduct, in the formulation and perpetuation of the dominant political theory, and in governing that major social unit, the family. Now, within less than ten years, two of the chief means by which Confucianism was maintained, the civil service examinations and the monarchy, had been swept away. With their disappearance Confucianism would be weakened, presumably fatally. Efforts were not lacking to maintain and revive it. For a time scholars trained under it kept up the traditional ceremonies in the Confucian temples which were familiar landmarks in every city and in some even of the modern schools. As we are to see, twice within the next decade attempts were made to restore the monarchy, one by Yüan Shih-k'ai himself and one which had as its object the renewal of the rule of the Manchu Dynasty. Yet both were short-lived. In that brief time China had moved too far away from the Confucian monarchy to permit its revival. Here and there, down to the triumph of Communism at midcentury, efforts were made to bring the republic to the support of Confucianism. In their ambitious endeavour in the 1930's to create a puppet state in Manchuria, the Japanese embarked on a somewhat similar attempt. By what is sometimes called 'social lag', much of Confucianism tended to persist in the customs and moral standards of the nation. The family, deeply indebted to Confucianism and incorporating much of its outlook, was an additional prop. Yet, for better or for worse, Confucianism was a waning factor in Chinese life. As it faded an ideological vacuum appeared. How would it be filled? Would it be by Christianity, by the liberal humanism of the Occident, by stark materialism, by nationalism, by a combination, possibly illogical, of all of these, or by some other ideology? By mid-century, as we are to see, Communism, which was not on the horizon in 1912, made what for the moment seemed a successful bid. Yet it was only a stage in the vast revolution into which the Chinese had been plunged and of which no man could foresee the outcome.

Inevitably the question obtrudes itself as to why, with the possible exception of Russia, by the mid twentieth century the cultural revolution brought by the impact of the Occident was more drastic in China than among any other people of high civilization. Russia had been captured by Marxist Communism, an ideology formulated in Western Europe, chiefly in London, but in spite of all its vast geographic extent it had less than half the population of China. Moreover, although in altered forms, much of the old Russia persisted, including its imperialistic ambitions. The tradition of rule by a dominant minority was maintained although the personnel and structure of the minority had changed. Russia was still 'Holy Russia', even though now it championed not a form of Christianity which it insisted was the only pure or orthodox version, but a Communism of which it claimed to be the authoritative interpreter. Outwardly greatly altered, China's near neighbour, Japan, more nearly preserved its inherited structure, with its imperial house, Shinto, and the military tradition. Ostensibly a republic, India kept more of its past, especially in religion and notably in Islam and in Hinduism with caste, the almost inseparable concomitant of Hinduism. No land where Islam was dominant was as greatly changed as China, neither Turkey, Iran, Pakistan, nor any of the Arab states. The answer is not clear. Perhaps there is no single answer. Possibly it lies in part in the realm of religion and in Confucianism itself. Certainly in Russia the Church proved more resistant than did Confucianism in China. Islam and Hinduism put up a more sturdy front. When Buddhism was dominant and was reinforced by nationalism, as in Ceylon, Burma, and Thailand, the changes were not as sweeping. In Japan it was the reverence for the Emperor, with its strong religious sanctions, and the strength of both Buddhism and Shinto which were in part accountable for the stability. But why was Confucianism so weak? Was it something in the nature of Confucianism? Or can it be that Confucianism was not as weak as it seemed and that more of it carried over in attitudes, disguised but still potent? The only honest reply is that we do not certainly know. The weakness seems to be a fact, but appearances may be deceptive. Even though we must confess ignorance, the question is of primary importance. In it may lie the clue to much of the future.

CHAPTER SIX

THE ATTEMPT AT A DEMOCRATIC REPUBLIC

IT was clear in 1912 to all but the most casual observers or the incorrigible optimists that China would have no easy course in the venture with a republic and democracy of a Western liberal type on which she had embarked. The area and population were huge, except possibly on the village level experience with that kind of government was utterly lacking, and the ideological basis on which Western democratic and republican institutions were erected, namely the Graeco-Roman background and Christianity, especially Protestant Christianity, was present only in small minorities. A generation later another land, India, with a population nearly as large and with a much greater diversity in culture and race, was to engage in a similar endeavour, but it had had the advantage of tutelage for nearly a century under British rulers, as experienced a people in democratic representative institutions as the world possessed.

Many factors entered into the Chinese scene and it was not at all clear what the outcome would be. One was the tradition of the strong man who had fought his way to the top, had restored unity and internal peace to the Empire, and, having done so, had become the progenitor of a new dynasty. Another factor, itself complex, was the influx of new political and social patterns from the Occident. Among them were democracy of the Anglo-Saxon type, constitutional monarchy, republican forms of government as exemplified by such varied countries as the United States and France, and socialism, including Marxist socialism, or Communism, which was not to come in force until the next decade. Chinese youth, freed from the cramping stereotypes of Confucianism which had constituted a strait-jacket to their elders, and open to all the winds of the earth, especially of the Occident, itself rapidly changing, now reached out eagerly in many directions in morals, in social practices, and in intellectual adventures. Intensely nationalistic and restive under discipline, Chinese students were to be reckoned with in politics, in relations with other nations, and in various aspects of intellectual, literary, artistic, and social life. Moreover, China was not permitted to work out her problems as though she were on a planet by herself. She was assailed by the fierce international competition of the age. Many nations sought a hand in her affairs. In the year 1912 European governments, as yet unweakened by the world wars which sapped their strength in the next third of a century, held leaseholds and other special privileges on her soil which compromised her economic, cultural, and political independence. Across the Pacific was the United States, officially benevolent and standing for the territorial and administrative integrity of China, and in doing so more and more concerned for the country and active in measures affecting that land. Nearer at hand was Japan, now become a continental power and with holdings in Manchuria, seeking to develop the markets and the natural resources of China for the benefit of her expanding industry and growing population. Then there was Russia, the colossus of the north, bordering on China through the longest land frontier on the planet. It had already absorbed more of the territory of the Chinese Empire than had any other existing foreign power and it continued to be intensely interested in China's internal affairs.

The main course of the political history for the forty years which followed 1912, though at first sight confusing, can in fact be rapidly summarized. First came an attempt of Yüan Shih-k'ai to make himself the master of all China, initially under the guise of the President of the Republic, combining the old with the new, and then frankly as the first Emperor of a new dynasty. In that he failed, and in 1916, after a little more than four years, he was eliminated by death on the eve of being liquidated by his critics. Then came a decade of turmoil, complicated by embroilment in World War I and

Japanese encroachments, encroachments which had begun before the death of Yüan Shih-k'ai. In that decade various 'war lords' fought and intrigued for the mastery of the Empire much after the manner in which, in earlier centuries at the end of a dynasty, warriors had struggled until one mastered the others and founded a new dynasty. Only now they were forced to pay lip-service to the idea of a republic. Early in the decade there was a twelve-day restoration of the Ch'ing Dynasty. Then, in 1926, the armies of the Kuomintang, or Nationalist Party, led by Chiang K'ai-shek, which had the programme of Sun Yat-sen as its guiding chart, began a triumphal progress which brought most of the country under their control. Here was a traditional strong man attempting to preserve something from Confucianism but seeking to rule through the machinery of a republic. The major domestic challenge came from the Communists, but they seemed in process of elimination. Distinct progress was being made towards unifying the country, towards creating a democratic structure of the kind familiar in the West, and towards freeing the country from the shackles imposed by foreign powers in Manchu times. Then the Japanese interfered, first beginning in the autumn of 1931 by trying to tear away Manchuria and much of Inner Mongolia in the form of a puppet state, and next, commencing in July 1937, with a full-scale invasion of all China. The struggle between China and Japan became a phase of World War II, when but for the aid of the United States the Nationalist Government would probably have been crushed. As it was, at the end of World War II, with the defeat of Japan, it was so badly weakened that it did not have the vitality to take advantage of its technical victory, to unify the country, and to meet the post-war economic problems. The Communists, who had grown in strength during the Japanese invasion, moved into the power vacuum and in 1949 and 1950 took possession and proceeded in alliance with Russia to essay the remaking of the country after their pattern. Their victory represented the triumph of Russia and of Russian totalitarian Communism over the liberalism and democracy of the West. The Nationalists retreated to Formosa, where they were protected by the United States. This is the outline which we are to develop more at length, noting as we do so the cultural changes and the relations with the rest of the world. In this chapter we will carry the story down to the beginning of the all-out attempt of Japan to subdue the country in July 1937.

We turn first, then, to the rule of Yüan Shih-k'ai. Yüan's election to the Provisional Presidency seemed to offer the most promising possibility of avoiding the continuation of debilitating civil war. He commanded the strongest army in the country and the official spokesmen for the republic acquiesced in his leadership. Yet there were deep cleavages which could be healed only by a combination of high statesmanship, tact, and vigour, and this Yüan, unfortunately, did not possess. In general, the vocal sentiment in the south was for the Republic and wished to move in the direction of liberal democracy of the kind found in Great Britain, Western Europe, and the United States. It found its chief expression through the Kuomintang, or Nationalist Party, an outgrowth of the T'ung Meng Hui, which was dominant in the Provisional National Assembly in Nanking. The north was more conservative and had in it many military men who were by no means committed to the Republic. Yüan's own conversion to it was superficial and from expediency. He did not really believe in it.

The struggle between the radical south, led by the Kuomintang, and Yüan Shih-k'ai began early. The former wanted the capital at Nanking. Yüan insisted that it be in Peking, and won. He induced the Provisional National Assembly to move to Peking. A provisional constitution, drafted by the Provisional National Assembly, was proclaimed on 10 March 1912, when Yüan was inaugurated. Under it a National Assembly or Parliament was elected in 1913. In it, too, the Kuomintang was potent. Friction inevitably ensued. A chief focus was the issue of a foreign loan. Money was needed to carry on the government, and current revenues were insufficient. The four-power consortium of foreign bankers now become, since Russia and Japan had insisted upon membership, a six-power combination, offered to provide it on condition that the income from the salt gabelle, long a source of income for the state, were assigned to its repayment. Since it had as a corollary increased foreign control, President Wilson refused the project the support of the United States and the American bankers withdrew. However, the five other powers persisted. Also alleging the further compromising of China's independence and unwilling to see Yüan partly freed, as he would be if the loan were consummated, from dependence on the national legislature for funds, the Kuomintang opposed ratification in the National Assembly. In the spring of 1913 Yüan forced the loan through, declaring that the earlier legislative body, the Provisional National Assembly, had approved it. Sun Yat-sen, who had been assigned what was to him the congenial task of planning a comprehensive programme for the development of railways for the entire Republic, hotly opposed the loan. In July he demanded that Yüan Shih-k'ai resign. A 'punitive expedition' to remove Yüan was projected in which four southern provinces joined. Yüan easily crushed it and Sun Yat-sen and several of the other leaders of the revolt fled to convenient Japan. The experience left Sun bitter against Yüan and the foreign money power. While living in obscurity in Japan, under an assumed name, Sun Yat-sen was much in the home of Charles Jones Soong, also a refugee from Yüan, and there it was that he entered into the marriage with one of the Soong sisters which we have already noted.

His success in crushing the 'punitive expedition' seemed to place Yüan Shih-k'ai firmly in power. He confirmed his position by forcing through the National Assembly (October 1913) his election as President for a five-year term. Accusing them of complicity in the summer's revolt, he then expelled from the Assembly the members of the Kuomintang, and a little later dismissed the remaining rump of that body. He also dissolved the provincial assemblies. In place of the National Assembly he brought together an Administrative

Conference of seventy men picked by himself. He also created a body elected on a limited franchise and made up of conservatives and moderates, to which was given the task of revising the provisional constitution. The document which it drafted lengthened the President's term to ten years and, in effect, gave him the power either to continue himself in office or to choose his successor. The President was accorded an absolute veto over actions of the parliament provided for by the constitution, and he was to appoint his own council of state. There was also a plan for drawing up a 'permanent' constitution, which was to be submitted to a national convention.

In 1915 Yüan Shih-k'ai went further and took steps to renew the Empire, with himself as the first of a new dynasty. He chose as a title for his reign Hung Hsien ('Great Constitutional Era'). In this step he was reinforced by the opinions of several advisers, one of them a distinguished American political scientist. Yet several of the foreign powers counselled against it. Moreover, opposition speedily developed, especially in the south. Advocates of the Republic resorted to arms. The first outbreak was in Yünnan, in the extreme south-west. Liang Ch'i-ch'ao, Minister of Justice in the cabinet, resigned in protest and retired to the safety of the foreign concessions in Tientsin and aided the Yünnan uprising. The revolt spread. On 22 February 1916, Yüan announced a postponement of the enthronement. A month later a decree declared that the monarchy had been cancelled and that Yüan would continue as President of the Republic. However, instead of allaying criticism, these steps, interpreted as symptoms of weakness, heightened it. Yüan was stripped of more and more power, the financial situation deteriorated, he became ill from a chronic disease aggravated by hard work, worry, and chagrin, and in June 1916 he died. The Vice-President, Li Yüan-hung, automatically succeeded to the Presidency.

The problems of Yüan Shih-k'ai and of China had in the meantime been complicated by developments in the international scene. Russia and Great Britain took advantage of

China's weakness to extend their influence in the outlying dependencies bordering on their possessions. Russia sought to draw Outer Mongolia into her orbit and to deal with it as independent of China. In 1915 China assented to Outer Mongolia's autonomy and to Russian commercial interests in the region in return for Russian acknowledgement of Chinese suzerainty over the area. Fearing Russian advance through Tibet towards India, Great Britain had sent an expedition to Lhasa, the capital, but Republican China refused to ratify a convention which would have recognized the British special interest in Tibet. In August 1914 what was eventually remembered as World War I broke out in Europe. Soon most of that continent was ablaze and the far-flung territories controlled by its powers were also affected. Great Britain, Russia, and France were embattled against Germany and Austria and within the next few months the conflagration spread. The Chinese Government wished to keep aloof from the conflict, declared its neutrality, and asked the belligerents to keep their hostilities out of its borders. It appealed to the United States to aid in persuading the warring powers to respect this wish. The United States acted, but cautiously, and China, still neutral, became deeply involved.

This involvement was due primarily to Japan. Those who led that country saw in the war a golden opportunity. Europe was too preoccupied within its own borders to offer effective opposition to Japanese ambitions. The Anglo-Japanese Alliance provided a convenient excuse. The British Government first sought to induce Japan to keep out of the conflict and then to confine its aid to naval assistance against German vessels in the China seas, but Japan was not to be deflected or restricted. She first demanded of Germany that the latter hand over to her the leasehold in Shantung, Kiaochow, 'with a view to eventual restoration of the same to China', a clause, incidentally, inserted at British insistence. When Germany did not reply, Japan (23 August 1914) declared war on Germany and promptly moved to seize Kiaochow. Both Germans and

Japanese, especially the latter, fought on Chinese soil with no respect for its neutrality, even after China, following its precedent in the Russo-Japanese War, attempted to define a war zone. Japan stormed Tsingtao, the city which dominated Kiaochow. In her military operations she also took possession of the German railways in Shantung and thus was in virtual control of that province.

Now followed, in January 1915, a set of twenty-one demands, in five groups, of Japan on China which, if granted, would have placed the Republic under the effective control, almost as a puppet, of its island neighbour. The first group had to do with Shantung and was designed to mark out that province as a Japanese sphere of influence. China was to promise to assent to any disposition which Japan might arrange with Germany on the future of the German rights in that province and Japan was to be permitted to build a railway in it. China was also to agree not to alienate any part of the province to a third power and was to open more ports in it. The second dealt with South Manchuria and Eastern Inner Mongolia. There the Japanese lease on Port Arthur and Dairen was to be extended from twenty-five to ninety-nine years and further exclusive privileges were to be granted to Japan and her citizens. The third group was intended to put under joint Japanese and Chinese control the Hanyehping iron works, a plant in the heart of China proper and the largest of its kind in the country. By the fourth group China was to covenant 'not to cede or lease to a third power any harbour or bay or island' along her coast, thus making all China in effect a Japanese sphere of influence. The fifth group was even more sweeping, and included the employment by China of Japanese advisers, the purchase from Japan of half or more of her munitions of war, the construction by Japanese of important railway lines in the Yangtze Valley, and the joint administration by Chinese and Japanese of the police in 'important places'. Sweeping as were these demands, they were but a foreshadowing of a much more breath-taking programe on which Japan was to embark in the 1930s and 1940s.

Japan straitly enjoined the Chinese Government to keep secret the content and even the existence of the demands, but inevitably the news leaked out. Of the major Western powers only the United States was sufficiently unentangled in war to protest. This she did, in correct diplomatic fashion, formally warning both Japan and China that she would not 'recognize any agreement or undertaking which has been entered into or which may be entered into between the Governments of Japan and China impairing the treaty rights of the United States and its citizens in China, the political or territorial integrity of the Republic of China, or the international policy relative to China commonly known as the Open Door policy'. Although beyond sending these notes she took no steps to enforce her position, the United States was further confirming a policy which in December 1941 was to involve her in war with Japan.

Under pressure, Japan seemed to retreat from most of the more extreme demands. On the first three groups China was constrained to yield, but not without important modifications in her favour. As to group four she more or less subtly checkmated Japan by a formal declaration that 'thereafter' she would not cede or lease any 'port, bay, or island' along her coast 'to any foreign power' – and in this Japan was obviously included. With one exception the obnoxious fifth group, so the Japanese said, was 'postponed for later negotiation'. When, as we are to see, it was renewed, it was not expressly as a renewal and was in altered and more sweeping forms. For some years May 9th, 1915, when China gave her formal assent, was annually commemorated by nationalistically-minded students as a day of humiliation.

World War I brought still further involvement and strain to China. In 1916 France began recruiting Chinese as labourers behind her lines and in 1917 Great Britain followed her example. Early in 1917, as the German pressure on them became more intense, Great Britain, France and Russia entered into secret agreements with Japan in which they promised to support at the peace conference her claim to the German holdings in Shantung and to the German islands in the Pacific north of the equator in return for Japanese naval help in the Mediterranean and for Japan's promise to urge China to break off diplomatic relations with Germany.

When, in February 1917 the United States severed its diplomatic relations with Germany, President Wilson sent a circular note to the other neutral countries, including China, suggesting that they do likewise. The American Minister to China urged on Li Yüan-hung and his associates that they act at once. Lansing, the American Secretary of State, was more cautious, and even when, in March, China complied, he advised against a Chinese declaration of war, fearing that this might plunge China into civil strife.

Lansing's fears were confirmed by the event. In April, 1917, the United States declared war on Germany. Should China follow? Japan was eager that China do so, seeing in that step and the loans and equipment needed to implement it, presumably to be had from Tokyo, a way of augmenting her influence in the Republic. The General Assembly or Parliament elected in 1913 had reconvened in Peking after the death of Yüan Shih-k'ai. In it the Kuomintang was the strongest element. It opposed China's entrance into the war, holding that Parliament should continue with its task of drafting a permanent constitution and that participation in the war would bring attempts at control by Japan. On the other hand, the Premier, Tuan Ch'i-jui, who had been Yüan Shih-k'ai's right hand man, and the cabinet dominated by him wished China to go to war with Germany. He summoned to Peking the tuchuns, the military commanders governing the several provinces. They joined with Tuan in favouring war. However, President Li Yüan-hung dismissed Tuan. Tuan took refuge in convenient Tientsin. There some of the tuchuns and other military men gathered and insisted that the President get rid of Parliament. To give point to their demand they declared the independence of the northern provinces of Peking and threatened to march on that city. Li Yüan-hung, weakening, complied and (14 June 1917) dissolved Parliament.

In need of military support, Li had called to his aid Chang Hsün and his army. Chang Hsün had come to prominence in the overturn of the Manchus and had under him a considerable force. On 1 July 1917, he electrified the world by restoring the Manchu boy Emperor and with him the Ch'ing Dynasty. In this he had the support of K'ang Yu-wei. He seems to have been actuated by the Confucian principle of loyalty of a minister to the prince. Li Yüan-hung asked the Vice-President, Fêng Kuo-chang, another military man, to take over the duties of President, recalled Tuan Ch'i-jui to the Premiership, and took refuge in the Japanese legation. Tuan and his friends among the military men were not minded to see the monarchy restored in this fashion with Chang Hsün in control. They marched on Peking, on 12 July 1917, Chang Hsün sought asylum in the Dutch legation, his troops were bought off by Tuan and his supporters, and the bewildered boy Emperor who, with his relatives, was an unwilling puppet in the entire affair, retired once more to his sanctuary in the imperial palace and his empty titles. The two fiascoes, that of Yüan Shih-k'ai and of Chang Hsün, had clearly made impossible the restoration of the Confucian monarchy.

Yet the country remained divided. The regime of Fêng Kuo-chang and Tuan Ch'i-jui (Li Yüan-hung, weary of public life and suffering from an enormous loss of face, refused to reassume the Presidency and retired to the safety of the foreign concessions in Tientsin) was regarded by the powers as the legitimate government of China and on 14 August 1917, declared war on Germany and Austria. Incidentally, in the complexities of Chinese politics, Liang Ch'i-ch'ao came out against his former mentor, K'ang Yu-wei, and sided with Tuan.

The Kuomintang leaders, unreconciled to the northern warlords, declared the dissolution of Parliament illegal, took refuge in Canton, and there set up what they insisted was the only constitutional government of the country. They centred it around the Parliament of 1913. Sun Yatsen joined them, for a time held the title of Generalissimo and then was a member of an administrative committee of seven. However, he was unable to work happily with the faction which hailed from the province of Kwangsi, and in 1919 he retired to the French Concession in Shanghai and there gave himself to writing and to waiting for a more favourable hour.

China's formal participation in the war against the Central Powers brought with it some real advantages but also embarrassing entanglements. She was able to cancel the portion of the Boxer indemnity due to Germany and Austria, obtained from the Entente powers a postponement of payments on that indemnity which were owed to them, and was assured of a seat at the peace conference. On the other hand she was in danger of falling under the control of Japan. In chronic need of money and confronted by a divided country, the factions ruling at Peking turned to Japan for financial and other assistance. Loans were obtained from Japan and to secure them liens were given on taxes, forests, mines, railways, and the telegraph system. A 'War Participation Board' was set up with a Japanese adviser and a contract was entered into with Japan for the supply of arms. There had been some hope of obtaining funds from American sources, but the United States Government, intent on winning the war against the Central Powers, subordinated its concern for China to that objective. Eager to allay friction with Japan, now its associate in that struggle, Washington arranged with Tokyo what was known as the Lansing-Ishii Agreement, so called from the two chief negotiators. By it both governments declared 'that territorial propinquity creates special relations between countries, and, consequently, the Government of the United States recognizes that Japan has special interests in China, particularly in the part to which her possessions are contiguous. The territorial sovereignty of China, nevertheless, remains unimpaired.' Moreover, both governments denied that they had ' any purpose to infringe in any way the indepenence or territorial integrity of China' and declared 'that they always adhere to the principle of the so-called "Open Door" of equal opportunity for commerce and industry in China ' and that they were 'opposed to the acquisition by any government of any special rights or privileges that would affect the independence or territorial integrity of China or that would deny to the citizens of any country the full enjoyment of equal opportunity in the commerce and industry of China'. To some Chinese the recognition that Japan had ' special interests in China' had a sinister sound and seemed to them to be a betrayal by the chief sponsor of the open door policy.

In 1917, 1918, and 1919 in the closing years of World War I and while the peace conference in Paris was attempting a settlement and to build a structure in the League of Nations which would prevent the recurrence of the holocaust, China appeared to be disintegrating internally. It was the era of the war lords when, but for the injection of the ideals of a republic and democracy, the struggle for power was in progress which would probably have ended in the founding of a new dynasty. A semblance of a central government was maintained at Peking which, fiction though it largely was, had the recognition of the powers. In 1918 Tuan Ch'i-jui and his group assembled a new Parliament which elected as President of the Republic a former official under the Manchu regime, Hsü Shih-ch'ang. In 1920 a group of war lords drove out Tuan and his group but left Hsü Shih-ch'ang in the Presidency, clearly a nominal and impotent figurehead. At that particular time the most powerful of the war lords was Chang Tso-lin, who had ruled in Manchuria since the revolution of 1911-12. Soft-spoken, looking like a scholar, he was completely ruthless. In Canton in that same year, 1920, a military man, a supporter of Sun Yat-sen, ousted the Kwangsi faction and Sun was once more in that city. A remnant of the Parliament of 1913 made its way back to Canton and in April 1921 elected Sun 'President of China'. China seemed to be falling apart into ephemeral and weak fragments.

In the meantime World War I had dramatically ended with the collapse of the Central Powers, preceded, a few months earlier, by a revolution in Russia which overthrew the Romanovs, ended the empire, and, late in 1917, was captured by the Bolshevik wing of the Communists. For a time it seemed that Japan would supplant Russia in the control of the railways in North Manchuria, but in this she was checkmated by the United States and until 1922 the roads were under an interallied commission headed by an American and on which China was given a voice.

When the peace conference assembled in Paris, China, as one of the belligerents, had a seat. Both the Peking and Canton regimes were represented on the delegation. The Chinese asked for the return to them of the former German properties and for abrogation of the Chino-Japanese treaties of 1915 and 1918 with their limitations on Chinese sovereignty. The abrogation of the treaties was held to be beyond the scope of the conference, but the Shantung properties became a burning issue. Japan argued that the secret agreements which she had with Great Britain, France, and Russia had promised them to her. At first the United States supported China, but eventually yielded, partly to prevent the conference from breaking up. The properties were awarded to Japan, but the latter's representatives said that all except the economic privileges in Shantung held by Germany and the right to a Japanese settlement in Tsingtao would eventually be returned to China. In protest the Chinese refused to sign the general treaty with Germany. However, they obtained membership in the League of Nations by signing the treaty with Austria and they negotiated a separate treaty with Germany.

Through the latter they won a cancellation of German extraterritorial privileges, thus making a breach in the solid wall of what they deemed the 'unequal treaties'. Austrian extraterritorial rights also disappeared.

The Paris settlement was intensely unpopular in China, and public opinion found expression through a boycott of Japanese goods and a student demonstration against the Anfu clique, the officials who were held to have sold out to the Japanese. When in 1920 Japan offered to open negotiations over the Shantung properties the offer was foiled by widespread distrust of acceptance as a possible admission of the legality of the award.

The change of governments in Russia brought some gains to China, but not all of them either immediately or permanently. Until 1920 Peking regarded the Tsarist diplomatic and consular officials as representing Russia. In November 1919 Peking withdrew its recognition of the autonomy of Outer Mongolia which had been given in 1915 under Russian pressure. In 1920 payments on the Russian share of the Boxer indemnity were discontinued. In 1919 the Communist Government in Russia made the conciliatory gesture of a rapprochement to China, offering to negotiate on the basis of the renunciation of extraterritorial rights and other special privileges, the restoration of territory taken from China under the Tsars, the cancellation of the Russian share in the Boxer indemnity, and the full control by China of the Chinese Eastern Railway, the line in North Manchuria. Since most of the Russians in China were 'white', adherents of the Tsarist regime, the surrender of extraterritorial privileges meant no sacrifice, but, rather, was a measure against these anti-Communists. When it came to the acid test of binding documents the U.S.S.R. was less yielding. In 1924 an agreement was signed which, while annulling the extraterritorial rights and the concessions obtained by Tsarist Russia and cancelling the Russian portion of the Boxer indemnity, provided that the latter should be used for education in China through a joint commission on which the Russian repre-

sentative had the veto power, and for the repurchase by
China, not the free gift from Russia, of the Chinese Eastern
Railway. Moreover, while the U.S.S.R. recognized Outer
Mongolia as 'an integral part of the Republic of China',
following the Tsarist policy it treated it as in fact autonomous and entered into direct negotiations with it. Moreover, the U.S.S.R., by-passing Peking, made a separate
agreement with Chang Tso-lin as the actual ruler of
Manchuria. Nor did the Soviets return the land taken
from the Ch'ing Dynasty; as soon as they were able they
tightened their control over the large section of Eastern
Siberia which had been given to Russia in the 1850's and
which for a time after 1917 had been in anti-Communist
hands.

China was deeply involved in what was known as the
Washington Conference, held in that city in 1921-2 on
invitation of the United States. The primary purpose of
the gathering was to remove the growing friction between
the United States and Japan over a naval armaments race
and other issues, including those in the Far East, which
threatened war. To it eight powers in addition to the United
States were asked because of their direct interest in the
questions discussed: Great Britain, Japan, France, Italy,
China, Belgium, the Netherlands, and Portugal, and a
comprehensive settlement was reached which for the time
allayed the tension. All the treaties which emerged from
the gathering affected China, some indirectly and others
directly. The fixing of the ratios of the strength of the
navies of the five larger powers together with the agreement
not to increase their fortifications on their island possessions
in the Western Pacific accorded to Japan what looked like
unchallengeable naval superiority in that region, and this
gave her not only what appeared to be security against
attack but also dominance over the sea approaches to
China. The four-power treaty which took the place of the
Anglo-Japanese Alliance whereby the British Empire,
France, Japan, and the United States agreed to respect one
another's insular possessions and dominions in the Pacific

was designed to ensure the *status quo* and thus further to remove the danger of a war in the Far East which might involve China. All nine powers signed a treaty in which among other measures they agreed 'to respect the sovereignty, the independence, and the territorial and administrative integrity of China; to provide the fullest and most unembarrassed opportunity to China to develop and maintain for herself an effective and stable government; to use their influence for the purpose of effectually establishing and maintaining the principle of equal opportunity for the commerce and industry of all nations throughout the territory of China; to refrain from taking advantage of conditions in China in order to seek special rights or privileges which would abridge the rights of subjects or citizens of friendly states, and from countenancing action inimical to the security of such states'. Moreover, provision was made for setting up a board of reference in China to inquire into the observance of this promise. Foreign postal agencies in China were to be discontinued, such foreign armed forces as were not specifically authorized by treaty or agreement were to be withdrawn 'whenever China shall assure the protection of the lives and property of foreigners in China', limitations were placed on foreign radio stations in China, and modifications of China's tariff duties were adopted which were designed to raise them and thus to increase China's revenue. The Chinese insistence on the removal of extraterritoriality won a promise from the powers to appoint a commission to investigate conditions and to relinquish extraterritorial rights 'when satisfied that the state of China's laws, the arrangements for their administration, and other considerations' warranted that step. Moreover, with certain conditions on the purchase by China of the former German railways, Japan returned to China Kiaochow and the other German properties in Shantung, and, while declining to accede to the Chinese request for the cancellation of the treaties of 1915 growing out of the twenty-one demands, agreed to withdraw completely the obnoxious fifth group which had been 'postponed for later negotiations'. In spite of her marked domestic weakness, through the Washington Conference China had made substantial gains towards freeing herself from the restrictions on her full autonomy which were so galling to her vocal elements.

The rising tide of Chinese nationalism soon brought additional pressure to annul the special position which foreigners enjoyed in China. In 1922 and again in 1924 an 'anti-religious', actually an anti-Christian movement accused Christian missions of being a phase of Western imperialism, berated missionaries, persecuted Christians as 'running dogs' of the foreigner, and insisted that the heads of institutions and the majority of the boards of management of educational institutions maintained by Christian bodies be Chinese. In 1925, whipped to frenzy by Communist agitation inspired in part from Russia, nationalist agitation against what were dubbed the 'unequal treaties' brought on violence and a boycott directed chiefly against the British. On May 30th of that year a strike in Shanghai led to a demonstration, largely by students, in the International Settlement. The police, British, arrested some of the agitators, and in self-defence fired into the crowd. 'May 30th' became a slogan and anti-British demonstrations, some of them violent, spread widely. On 23 June 1925, a clash occurred in Shameen, the foreign settlement in Canton, because of a Chinese attempt to rush into it. The boycott proved very costly to British merchants. As we are to see in a moment, the movement against Western 'imperialists' reached a peak in 1926 and 1927 in connexion with the association of the Communists with the revived Kuomintang.

It was not only in the political realm that the revolution was being seen. As we have suggested, it was especially potent among students. In them it was prominent in the intellectual, moral, religious, and social aspects of life. Schools of Western types continued to multiply and were thronged. From time to time, to the neglect of scholarship, students were absorbed in political agitation both on the domestic level and in foreign affairs. But they were vibrant with life. Efforts were made by mass education to raise the literacy level of the rank and file of the population.

Students flocked abroad in ever increasing numbers. The totals in Japan tended to fluctuate with the state of Chinese sentiment towards that country. Of those who sought in the Occident the sources of the new learning, the majority still went to the United States. After World War I numbers were on the Continent of Europe, especially in France. 'Returned students' augmented the flow of change, bringing in a wide variety of convictions which reflected the differing currents in the lands where they had been. Many were impressed by the democracy of the United States. After World War I some on the Continent of Europe began to imbibe Communism. English was the foreign language most studied. This was in large part because of the long British dominance in the foreign commerce of the land. It was also furthered by Protestant mission schools, most of which were British or American. One of the most striking phases of the intellectual revolution was the use of the vernacular and the spread of one form of the vernacular over China. Traditionally scholars had looked with disdain on the vernacular and serious works were in the classical style. However, some of the younger scholars who won a wide following among the rising generation began to write in the *pai hua*, the speech of the people. The leader in this movement was Hu Shih who, trained in the old learning in a family with scholarly traditions, after making a brilliant record in American universities, chiefly in philosophy, returned to China and became outstanding as a teacher and writer. It is from a manifesto which he put forth on 1 January 1917, that the wide use of the *pai hua* is usually dated. The *pai hua* was a dignified Mandarin, the most widely spoken form of the vernacular. As the *kuo yü*, or 'national speech', it began to be taught in the schools throughout the land and thus increasingly became familiar in the areas, notably along the coast south of Shanghai, where the multitude of dialects had long been a handicap to national unity. More and more the *pai hua* was the vehicle for younger writers.

Associated with the widening use of the *pai hua* was what was known as the 'New Tide', 'Renaissance', or 'New Thought'. It was a name given to the movement by which the Chinese mind, emancipated from the patterns long imposed by Confucian orthodoxy, was reaching out in many directions and flowing in a diversity of channels, some old and from China's past, some Occidental, and some quite new. Interest in several of China's philosophers, such as Mo Ti, long looked at askance by the orthodox, was revived. Many of the ideologies and the schools of thought in the Occident had their advocates in China. Bertrand Russell and John Dewey visited China in 1919 and 1920 and lectured in the most pulsing centre of the intellectual awakening, Peking University. Dewey especially made a deep impression. Some Chinese writers were venturing out in ways which had no exact parallels in either China's past or the Occident.

In social customs and in morals youth was experimenting. The sharp separation of the sexes was disappearing and boys and girls, young men and women, were being educated together and were mixing freely socially, sometimes with scant regard for the ethical standards of the past. Against ancient custom many were insisting on arranging their own marriages. There were domestic tragedies brought on by the marriage in the traditional fashion of girls trained in the old manner to boys who had been educated abroad or in the modern schools of China. Some of the familiar forms of etiquette fell into disuse. Western dress was widely adopted, though from time to time waves of nationalism brought a resurgence of Chinese styles.

In religion, not only Confucianism but also Taoism and Buddhism declined, and though in some parts of the country there was a revival of Buddhism, on the whole the waning of that faith which had been in progress since the T'ang Dynasty continued. Yet the numbers of Christians continued to mount, and in the decade between 1914 and 1924 the increase in Roman Catholics was fully 50 per cent and of Protestants between 60 and 70 per cent. By the mid-twenties each of the great wings of the Church was taking steps to transfer leadership to the Chinese and was achieving a nation-wide organization. Nevertheless, while their influence was far greater than their numbers would have seemed to warrant, in 1924 Christians of all varieties totalled only about three millions, or less than one out of every hundred of the population.

In spite of the vitality in many aspects of China's life and of progress in freeing the country from the 'unequal treaties' with their encroachments on China's independence, by the mid-twenties China seemed to be approaching a nadir of internal disunity and chaos. Most of the country was ruled by war lords, some controlling thousands of square miles and more than one province, and others only small areas. Banditry was rife. The Central Government had less and less authority. In 1922 one of the war lords, Wu P'ei-fu, defeated his chief rival, Chang Tso-lin. He sought to unite the country by recalling to Peking the Parliament of 1913 and to the Presidency Li Yüan-hung, thus giving the Republic the men under whom it had last been most nearly united. However, the following year the revolt of one of Wu P'ei-fu's subordinates, the 'Christian general', Fêng Yü-hsiang, a vigorous and somewhat enigmatic figure, made Li Yüan-hung consider his position impossible and he retired to the calm of his home in a foreign concession in Tientsin. Another war lord, Ts'ao Kun, bought his way to the Presidency by heavy bribes and in October 1923 what was optimistically hailed as a 'permanent' constitution was promulgated. In 1924 a combination of the forces of Fêng Yü-hsiang and Chang Tso-lin removed Ts'ao Kun from office and imprisoned him and put Tuan Ch'i-jui at the head of the state as Provisional Chief Executive. In 1926 Wu P'ei-fu and Chang Tso-lin combined their forces and drove Fêng Yü-hsiang out of Peking. Tuan Ch'i-jui thereupon retired, as had Li Yüan-hung, to the convenient haven of

Tientsin. China now did not have even a nominal chief executive and rapidly shifting cabinets tolerated by the dominant war lords were the only semblance of a Central Government. The powers dealt with the cabinet as representing China, but no one was deceived.

Then from the south came a new force in the form of a revived Kuomintang, which within less than two years brought much of the country together, gave it a regime stronger than it had had since the latter part of the nineteenth century, and until the Japanese struck at it seemed to be on the way to leading China out of the confusion and anarchy of the recent decades into a government which would combine some of the Confucian tradition with liberal democratic ideals derived from the West but modified to meet the Chinese situation. For the most of the time after April 1921, when, as we have seen, what was left of the Parliament of 1913 had elected him 'President of China', Sun Yat-sen had maintained a precarious foothold in Canton. To be sure, in 1922 he had to flee to escape the efforts of one of his followers to eliminate him, but early in 1923 he was back in the city. There he was wooed by representatives of Communist Moscow and, declaring himself disillusioned with the West, he turned his face towards Russia. He did not become a Communist, but he was willing to accept Russian advice in the reorganization of the Kuomintang. Through these counsellors, notably Borodin, that party was given a structure which resembled that of the Communist Party of Russia. This was furthered by what was called the First National Congress of the Kuomintang, convened in Canton in January 1924. A pattern was adopted through which the Kuomintang mapped out an organization which included units on the local level and which rose in a pyramid through district and provincial bodies to one on the national level that co-ordinated and dominated the rest. Through its constitution Sun Yat-sen was accorded a virtual dictatorship of the party. His writings became authoritative. Especially emphasized was his *San Min Chu I* ('The Three People's Leading Principles'). They could be roughly summarized and translated as the People's Nationalism (meaning that China must be freed from control by foreigners and acquire true national unity), the People's Government (or Democracy), and the People's Livelihood (or Socialism – although Sun Yat-sen differed decidedly from Marx).

Sun laid out a programme for achieving democracy which was to have three stages. The first of these was to be that of a purely military government, the second was to be one of political tutelage under the party during which the citizens would learn self-government, and the third was to be the culmination of the process in a constitutional regime under a written document with a popularly elected Parliament and President. In place of the division of powers which he observed in the governments of the Occident, namely, executive, legislative, and judicial, Sun envisioned one of five powers in which should be included the three familiar in the West but to which should be added two others taken over and adapted from China's past, namely, one for examinations through which all officials were to be screened, and one for censorship or control. After his death, Sun Yat-sen's farewell message to China in the form of a will was especially revered.

Sun Yat-sen died in Peking on 12 March 1925, of cancer of the liver, after an operation some weeks earlier in a Christian hospital, that of the Peking Union Medical College, had disclosed the disease to be incurable. He had gone north on invitation from such government as existed in Peking for a conference hopefully designed to unite the country. Born in 1866, he was not yet sixty when with his demise he became the most influential man in the nation.

Sun's death was a boon to the Kuomintang. It relieved it of his control, for Sun, a dreamer and a revolutionary, was not a practical administrator. It also gave to the party and to the country a national hero whose role was not unlike that of Lenin in Communist Russia. His death, too, came at a time when the Kuomintang, reorganized and with a programme, was in a position to make a successful bid for power.

The bid for power was made in the traditional Chinese fashion, through an army and an able general. The leader was Chiang Kai-shek (or Chiang Chieh-shih). He was born in 1887 in the province of Chekiang, of sturdy but humble stock. His mother, although widowed when he was a child and with a family to rear, saw to it that he had an opportunity for an education, at first in the traditional Confucian curriculum. In his 'teens Chiang determined to follow a military career, and for that purpose he attended first the National Military Academy in Paotingfu, in the north, and then, from 1907 to 1911, the Tokyo Military Staff College. He also early became committed to the cause of revolution and while in Japan was a member of Sun Yat-sen's T'ung Meng Hui. When, in October 1911, the revolution in China broke out, he left Japan and joined the republican army in Shanghai. On the failure of the 'punitive expedition' against Yüan Shih-k'ai in 1913, Chiang Kai-shek joined Sun Yat-sen in Japan. Later he was back in China, for a time in Shanghai and occasionally with Sun Yat-sen as a companion in the latter's vicissitudes in Canton. As a representative of Sun he was in Russia in 1923 to study the situation, especially in its military aspects, but soon he was back in Canton, and there, with the authorization of Sun Yat-sen and under the counsel of Russian Communist advisers, he founded and became the first head of the Whampoa Military Academy. In this institution, of which Chiang was exceedingly proud, were trained many of the later officers of the armies of the Kuomintang, and through it he was able to rise to the command of those armies and to begin to display some of the leadership and the military skill which were to mark the next years of his career.

In the bid for power made by the Kuomintang through its armies under the generalship of Chiang Kai-shek the Communists had an important place. Very soon after a revolution in 1917 brought the Bolshevik wing of the Communists to power in Russia some of the Chinese intellectuals became interested in it. In Peking University members of the faculty, Ch'ên Tu-hsiu and Li Ta-chao, believing that traditional Chinese culture was bankrupt, began searching for a substitute. Ch'ên was inclined to favour the kind of liberalism exemplified in the West by the Manchester school. Li was more metaphysical. In the spring of 1918, at the instance of Li and composed mainly of students, a group was formed to study Marxism. In this group and himself a student was Mao Tse-tung.

Mao Tse-tung, later to be the outstanding figure in Chinese Communism, was born in 1893, the son of a prosperous farmer in Hunan, the province from which had come Tsêng Kuo-fan and Tso Tsung-t'ang. His early education was in the traditional classical style, but later he was in schools of the modern type. He was an enthusiast for the revolution of 1911. He came under the influence of the writings of K'ang Yu-wei and Liang Ch'i-ch'ao, then discarded them for those of Hu Shih and Ch'ên Tu-hsiu, and described his mind later as being in his mid-twenties a compound of anti-militarism, anti-imperialism, liberalism, democratic reformism, and Utopian Socialism. From Changsha, the capital of Hunan, where he graduated from a normal college in 1916, he went to Peking University, where to support himself he became assistant librarian. Returning to Hunan in 1919, he engaged actively in political agitation and began to organize labourers, but it was not until the summer of 1920, and after a second visit to Peking and a reading of Communist literature, that he became a convinced Marxist.

By September 1920 Ch'ên Tu-hsiu had come to the conviction that democracy as Dewey presented it and as seen in Britain and the United States was too slow for the needs of China, and had become captivated by Marxism-Leninism as promising early and complete transformation not only for China but also for the world. Not far from the same time Li Ta-chao also went over to Marxism, but by way of a social Darwinism. Ch'ên and Li carried with them many students who had been accustomed to look to them for leadership. In 1920 Ch'ên organized a group in Shanghai, and Li one in Peking, neither of them strictly Communist.

It was under the guidance of a Comintern Russian agent that from these groups and around these men the Chinese Communist Party sprang into being and in 1921 held its first national congress. Ch'ên Tu-hsiu became the first chairman of its Central Committee and attended the fourth congress of the Comintern in Moscow in November 1922. Li Li-san, a former student in Paris, where it may have been that he became a convert to Communism, and who in 1927 was to displace Ch'ên and who was later to be a rival of Mao Tse-tung, came to the fore as the organizer of a Communist-led labour union in the great iron works in Hanyang, in Central China.

The Chinese Communist Party co-operated with the Kuomintang, especially after the latter was reorganized by Russian advice on the pattern of the Communist Party of Russia. This seems to have been at the command of the Comintern and for the purpose of capturing the Kuomintang and thus winning China, a Russian Communist procedure which was to become the pattern in country after country. At its first congress, held in Canton in January 1924, the Kuomintang adopted as policies alliance with the U.S.S.R. and the Chinese Communist Party and support for the workers and peasants. When the Whampoa Military Academy was founded in May 1924, in addition to having Chiang Kai-shek as President, it had Chou En-lai as head of its political department, to see that the cadets were indoctrinated with revolutionary views. Chou was later to come to prominence in the Chinese Communist state. The son of an official of the old regime, the foundations of his education were traditional, in Confucianism. But he also had been a student in one of China's best modern schools, had studied in France, England, and Germany, and in 1921 in Paris had helped organize a branch of the Chinese Communist Party. His wife, also a Communist, had been one of the earnest girl students who had wholeheartedly embraced the radical views of the new day. When in 1926 the army of the Kuomintang, led by Chiang Kai-shek, moved northward, it was with the approval of the Comintern and

Borodin. To it military supplies were shipped from the U.S.S.R. by way of Vladivostok. Communist strength was augmented by Chinese students returning from Moscow, for in 1925 the Russians had set up there a university named after Sun Yat-sen, and by the end of 1927 it had an enrolment of about 600, most of them from the provinces of Kwangtung and Hunan.

The northward march of Chiang Kai-shek, although not without some hard fighting, was at first strikingly successful. It was into what in effect was a political vacuum and through a region which was weary of war lords, bandits, and civil strife. It was aided by propagandists and organizers of workers who held out Utopian hopes of high wages and better labour conditions and encouraged labourers to make exorbitant demands on employers and to be especially rebellious against foreigners as 'imperialists'. Little well-organized opposition was encountered and by the spring of 1927, marching northward down the Hsiang River in Hunan, Chiang Kai-shek had taken such important cities as Changsha, Wuchang, and Hankow, and then, turning eastward, had become master of Shanghai, the main commercial, industrial, and financial centre of China. In the north armies sympathetic with the Kuomintang seemed to be winning.

In the course of the northward advance the alliance between Chiang Kai-shek and the Communists had been strained by dissensions. Soon it broke down. In the capital of the Kuomintang regime set up in Hankow radical anti-imperialist and Communist elements were strong. For a time it looked as though they might prevail. Early in 1927 they and their sympathizers were in control. The British concessions in Hankow and Kiukiang were seized by mobs and the British marines withdrew rather than provoke a recurrence of the 30 May 1925 incident with its subsequent wave of anti-British activity. In Shanghai in the spring of 1927 successful strikes among the workers in the factories fomented by the Communists or their collaborators seemed to have prepared the way for the taking over of the city by organized labour. In March 1927 an army of pro-Communist troops took possession of Nanking, roughly handled foreigners, killed some of them, and would have killed more had not gunboats of the powers laid down a timely barrage around the house in which many had taken refuge. Vigorous anti-imperialist, anti-capitalist, anti-landlord forces seemed to be having their way. However, there were weakening factions in the Chinese Communist Party. Ch'ên Tu-hsiu, for instance, had never been reconciled to the alliance with Chiang Kai-shek and the Kuomintang. In Moscow there was by no means complete agreement on what should be done in China. Stalin and Trotsky, for example, were at variance, the former favouring co-operation with the Kuomintang and the latter wishing to keep the Communist Party entirely free from it. Chiang Kai-shek and some of the moderates in Kuomintang were also unhappy over the radical measures of the extremists. As early as March 1926 Chiang had nipped in the bud a Communist plot in Kwangtung, had removed several Communists from key posts, and had dissolved a strike committee in Hongkong. Immediately after the Nanking incident of March 1927 Chiang Kai-shek rushed to Shanghai to prevent a repetition of it in that city, presumably partly because he feared foreign intervention on a large scale if in that major centre of foreign population that act of violence was emulated. He assumed full responsibility for what had taken place in Nanking and then, with the help of conservative Chinese elements in Shanghai, including secret societies, he dissolved the labour unions and suppressed Communist activities in that city. He also had similar measures taken in Hangchow, which seemed about to be seized by the Communists and their sympathizers. He established his headquarters at Nanking, apart from the radical centre at Hankow.

For a time it looked as though both Communism and the Kuomintang would be ruined by the break. The government at Hankow disintegrated. Borodin fled the country and lived in Moscow, out of favour with his superiors because of the failure attributed to him. Some of the Chinese Communists and their sympathizers, took refuge in Russia, among them the Soong daughter who was the widow of Sun Yat-sen. Ch'ên Tu-hsiu lost his place as the head of the Chinese Communist Party, and within a few months Li Li-san was in the ascendant. In various parts of the country conservatives among the Chinese hunted down Communists and killed them. For instance, that was done by Chang Tso-lin, at that time master of Peking. In August 1927 Chiang Kai-shek resigned his command and sought out the quiet of a Buddhist temple near his boyhood home, but not until he had issued a manifesto calling upon the Kuomintang to sever all ties with the Communists, to complete the revolution and, moving north, to take Peking. More than one of the war lords seized the opportunity of the break between the Kuomintang and the Communists and the retirement of Chiang to regain some of the ground which they had lost.

Chiang Kai-shek could not long remain in retirement. In his temple retreat he was sought out by a throng of visitors. He seemed indispensable if the Kuomintang were to recover and win. In the months of his retirement he married, like Sun Yat-sen, as a second wife a daughter of the Soong family. Both she and he first went to Japan to win the consent of her mother, now a widow and living in that country. By that marriage Chiang became allied with an able American-educated son of that family, T. V. Soong, and with H. H. Kung, a descendant of Confucius, also American-educated, a Protestant Christian, and the husband of another of the Soong sisters. Before many months, with these three men in high offices, there was gossip of the 'Soong Dynasty'. Shortly, moreover, but not as a condition of his marriage and apparently from sincere motives, Chiang asked and was given baptism into the Methodist form of the Christian faith, that of the Soong family. In January 1926 Chiang Kai-shek returned to Nanking, once more at the head of the Kuomintang armies and clearly the strongest man in the Kuomintang.

Back in command, Chiang Kai-shek pushed the project

of unifying the country under the Kuomintang as against the Communists and through winning the north, especially Peking, symbolic as it was of the mastery of China. First the Nationalist Government, as we must call that set up by the Kuomintang, broke with the U.S.S.R., having as an additional incentive the seizure of Canton, the erstwhile centre of the Kuomintang, by Communists in December 1927. Since the Russian consulate had been implicated in the uprising, when the Nationalist forces retook the city it was closed. Moreover, all the Russian consulates in territories controlled by the Nationalists were shut and all representatives of the U.S.S.R. were forced out. The break with Russia and the Communists was complete. The enmity between the Communists and Chiang Kai-shek was reinforced. Moreover, a settlement was made with the powers, first with Great Britain and the United States, of the issues arising from the Nanking incident. Chiang and his armies now moved rapidly northward. In this they were assisted by Fêng Yü-hsiang and Yen Hsi-shan, the latter the war lord in control of the province of Shansi since the revolution which overthrew the Manchus. In June 1928 the Nationalist forces entered Peking. Chang Tso-lin, while on his train retreating to Manchuria, was killed by a bomb set by a plot of young officers in the Kwantung Army, the Japanese force stationed in Manchuria. Apparently they believed that in removing him they would facilitate the extension of Japanese control in that region. Chang Tso-lin was succeeded by his son, Chang Hsüeh-liang, who was not as strong a man as his father but who proved even less amenable to the Japanese than had he.

In theory, and to a large extent in practice, China was now united. The military stage of the revolution as envisaged by Sun Yat-sen had been brought to a conclusion. Certainly the country was more nearly one than at any time since the first months of the Presidency of Yüan Shih-k'ai, and perhaps even more so than then.

Yet that union was by an uneasy combination of various elements and was by no means complete. The strongest man was Chiang Kai-shek. He was committed to the ideals and to much of the programme of Sun Yat-sen, but, as we have suggested, he also represented the tradition by which dynasties had earlier been created, namely, the rule of a military man who had emerged on top after a struggle with his rivals. There were other military men whom he had not yet eliminated and each of whom, although giving lip-service to the revolution and the Kuomintang, was master of a region and of an army and must be placated, wooed, or destroyed. For the moment most of them were willing to co-operate.

The Kuomintang provided the structure through which unity was undergirded. Sun Yat-sen's stage of tutelage under a single party was now officially described as having arrived. The Kuomintang extended its organization until it became almost nation-wide. In the large majority of the local administrative units it had what was usually called a *tangpu*, an executive committee of the party members, and at the top level there was the National Congress. That body met infrequently and in the interim was represented by the Central Executive Committee. The Central Executive Committee controlled the national government. This, it will be recognized, was a conscious adaptation of a Russian prototype which had earlier been devised through the counsel of Communists from Moscow. Within the Kuomintang were several factions, in principle centring around theories but actually chiefly around persons.

The national government professed to conform to the pattern bequeathed by Sun Yat-sen. It had five main divisions, executive, legislative, judicial, examining, and control, each represented by what was called a *yüan*. Over them and co-ordinating them was a President and a Council of State of from twelve to sixteen members. There were also provincial governments. Officially the whole was called the National Government of the Republic of China. Sun Yat-sen was revered as the hero of the revolution, the party, and the nation. His writings, especially his *San Min Chu I* and his will, were officially proclaimed as providing the programme for the nation. The *San Min Chu I* was studied in the schools, and weekly the will was read in them. Weekly, too, students and teachers bowed before Sun's portrait and the flag of the Republic, observed three minutes of silence and meditation, and sang the party song.

The capital was established at Nanking. This had been the wish of Sun Yat-sen. Moreover, it was nearer the industrial and financial heart of China than was Peking and, in contrast with the latter, the foreign legations would not be like a fortress defended by foreign troops, and thus the capital would be freed from that chronic reminder of China's weakness before the powers. On Purple Mountain, overlooking the city, a stately tomb was erected for Sun Yat-sen, and to it his body was brought with great pomp. The city throbbed with life as buildings for the various government agencies arose and officials and those eager for office flocked to it. Peking was renamed Peiping ('Northern Peace').

Under the regime thus set up in Nanking a new and happier day seemed to have dawned for the troubled country. In its employ were many of the students of the modern schools in China and of those who had returned from study in Japan, the British Isles, the continent of Europe, and the United States. It had the support of most of the substantial elements, especially of the merchants, manufacturers, and bankers of Shanghai. Advance was registered in several aspects of the nation's life.

The Nationalist regime was not yet fully master of the country. As we shall see in a moment, the Communists challenged it. Moreover, in some sections banditry was prevalent. Here and there a war lord was restive. In 1930 two of the strongest of them, Fêng Yü-hsiang and Yen Hsi-shan, joined in attacking Chiang Kai-shek. Yet they were worsted and Chiang and the Kuomintang were stronger than ever. The latter seemed to be winning in the struggle for the unity and control of China.

Important gains were made in freeing China from the restrictions which had been imposed on its sovereignty in the later days of the Manchus and in the first years of the Republic. They were part of a wider revolt of subject peoples against the rule of the Occident, which had been accelerated by World War I and which was seen especially in Asia and its fringing islands and in Africa. Before 1927 most of the powers had remitted the unpaid portions of their share of the Boxer indemnity, although never without designating the purpose towards which they were to be used. It was in 1930 that the cancellation of Great Britain's leasehold on Weihaiwei, promised at the Washington Conference in 1922, was finally accomplished. In addition to the foreign concessions in the ports which were regained before 1928, several others were returned to China after that year, among them those held by the British in Chinkiang and Amoy. Chinese were admitted to membership in the councils which governed the International Settlements in Shanghai and Kulangsu (an island off Amoy) and the French Concession in Shanghai. On 1 January 1927, the Mixed Court in Shanghai, in which Chinese defendants were tried and which had been taken over by the foreign consuls in 1911, was restored to the Chinese. In 1928 and 1929 most of the Western powers, and in 1930 Japan, agreed to the resumption of tariff autonomy by China. On 1 February 1929, a schedule of customs duties fixed by China came into effect. The duties were still collected by the Customs Service which had been organized by Hart. That administration, preserved practically intact during the years of China's division, helped to give a degree of unity to the country. However, additional foreigners were not taken on the staff and Chinese were raised to the higher ranks. In the 1920s treaties providing both for tariff autonomy and for the surrender of extra-territorial rights were signed with a number of countries, including, as we have seen, such important ones as Germany and Russia. As other treaties expired China notified their holders that new ones would be negotiated only on the basis of equality and reciprocity, and by 1928 over half the foreigners living in China, if Koreans (who were Japanese subjects) were excepted, had no extra-territorial privileges. Great Britain, France, Japan, and the

United States retained theirs, but in December 1929 China announced that by her unilateral action all extraterritoriality would be terminated on the first day of the next month. However, the implementation of the action was postponed for two years. Before that date had arrived Japanese aggression in Manchuria, which we are to recount a little later, led to further delay.

Moreover, foreign powers were less inclined to use armed force to emphasize their demands or to protect their citizens than they had been in the nineteenth century or earlier in the twentieth century.

In Manchuria immigration was making the region more solidly Chinese than at any earlier time. The Manchus had attempted to keep it, their homeland, as a preserve for themselves. Yet under the pressure of population south of the Great Wall millions of Chinese moved northward into its comparatively vacant lands. Especially after the coming of the Republic, Chinese poured in, so that here was the greatest migration anywhere on the planet during those years. Whatever its political connexions might be, Manchuria was indisputably Chinese in population.

Yet China was by no means fully emancipated from foreign encroachments on its territories and its autonomy. As we have seen, some of the major powers retained their extraterritorial privileges, in Peking the legations preserved the semi-fortress status which had been theirs since the Boxer outbreak, and the largest city and chief port and financial centre, Shanghai, was built around the International Settlement and the French Concession. Foreign gunboats continued to traverse the inland waters of China, especially the Yangtze, to protect their nationals. Steamboats were multiplying, more and more of them owned by Chinese, but foreign firms still operated the majority of the larger ships along the coasts and in the Yangtze Valley. Moreover, and ominously, Japan maintained her leaseholds, railways, mines, and factories in South Manchuria and was intent on developing her interests there.

In North Manchuria the Russians, in spite of their fair

professions, kept their hold on the Chinese Eastern Railway. Relations between the Nationalist Government, Chang Tso-lin, and Chang Hsüeh-liang on the one hand and Russia on the other were far from friendly. In July 1929 the Chinese took matters in their own hands, seized the Chinese Eastern Railway, and dismissed and arrested the Russian officials. Moscow retaliated and, in spite of efforts by Henry L. Stimson, the Secretary of State of the United States, who called attention to the Pact of Paris, by which Russia and China along with other powers had renounced 'recourse to war for the solution of international controversies' and 'as an instrument of national policy in their relations with one another,' what was in reality a state of war existed for several months, and early in 1930 a Russian invasion restored the traditional Russian hold on the line. However, in December 1932 regular diplomatic relations were established between the U.S.S.R. and the Nationalist Government.

In spite of these survivals of foreign infringements on Chinese sovereignty, under the Nationalist Government of the Kuomintang China was clearly forging ahead. New railways were being built and others were projected. Automobiles were multiplying not only in the cities but also in the countryside. Passenger transportation was increasingly by auto-buses. While they were usually overcrowded and most of the roads which they traversed were execrable, they were popular and helped to make the population more mobile and to enhance national unity. The aeroplane was introduced and air lines were established. Factories multiplied. Many of them were for the manufacture of cotton textiles. As a result the purchase of foreign cotton yarn and cloth declined sharply from nearly a third of the total imports in 1913 to less than 10 per cent in 1931 and 1932. The importation of kerosene, used chiefly for lighting purposes, nearly trebled between 1900 and 1929. In the 1920's imports also had as major items tobacco, for the now ubiquitous cigarette, and manufactured metal products, especially machinery – an indication of the mounting industrialization. Opium, once the major import, was still brought in, but illicitly and largely in the form of morphine and heroin. Raw cotton for the factories and foodstuffs were prominent among the imports, the latter an indication that China, although predominantly agricultural, was not raising enough on its land to feed its swollen population. Exports were chiefly of raw or partially finished materials. Among them tea and silk were still seen, but as minor items in contrast with their supremacy a century earlier. Among the more considerable items of export were vegetable oils, bean cake, hair, furs, antimony, and cotton goods and thread. China was still buying more than she sold. The difference was made up chiefly by remittances to their families from overseas Chinese, expenditures by foreign travellers and armed forces, and sums sent in by Christian missionary agencies.

However, foreign commerce was still much less than the size of the country and its population would have led the casual observer to expect. Industrial development by Western processes, while increasing, was handicapped by lack of capital and by the fear of insecurity from civil strife, which discouraged capital investments. Most of the industry of the land was through the traditional handicrafts. Yet the guilds by which industry and commerce had been organized were disappearing, replaced by labour unions and chambers of commerce.

The patterns of trade were being altered. Not as much as formerly was the import and export business in the hands of foreigners. More Chinese firms were engaging in it. The old-fashioned comprador through whom the foreigner dealt with his Chinese customers was disappearing and direct contact was becoming the rule. In spite of the confusion in the currency, a confusion which was not remedied by the Nationalist regime, Chinese banks on Western models were multiplying and foreign banks no longer filled so large a place in the financial scene.

Great Britain continued to lead European countries in its share of the overseas trade, and Hongkong, a British crown colony, was, as formerly, a major centre of commerce, an intermediary between China and the West. Yet late in the 1920's in total commerce with China Japan surpassed Great Britain. Before 1930 the United States had also a larger proportion of China's commerce than Britain, and in 1932 it forged ahead of Japan. The proportion of trade passing through Hongkong declined from over a fourth in 1913 to less than a tenth in 1932. Yet if all the British Commonwealth be taken together, its trade with China still surpassed that of Japan, the British remained strong in the Customs Service, and outside of Manchuria the Hongkong and Shanghai Banking Corporation, British owned and operated, was, as it had been for many years, the strongest financial institution in China.

The intellectual ferment persisted. Schools of the modern type teaching primarily the learning of the Occident increased in numbers and enrolments. Students were intensely interested in politics, both national and international, and from time to time organized to make their convictions effective. Movements to promote the literacy of the masses continued. The *pai hua* came increasingly into use by the intellectuals, and the *kuo yü*, taught in the schools, was more and more understood in the regions of a multiplicity of dialects. Newspapers, magazines, and less ephemeral literature mounted in volume.

Confucianism was still declining. Chiang Kai-shek attempted to reinvigorate its morality. Through what was called the New Life Movement, launched in February 1934, he sought to renew such ancient Chinese virtues as courtesy, devotion to the public welfare, cleanliness, honour, and the hatred of all evil. Yet this reform movement lacked effective popular roots. In a few centres there was a continuation of the revived study of Buddhism, but that faith was moribund. Taoism was even more in decay. The Christian churches continued their growth and both Roman Catholics and Protestants sought to develop Chinese leadership and advanced it rapidly in the administration of the churches and the related educational and other institutions. Yet Christians were only about 1 per cent of the population.

Hopeful though the outlook seemed to be for a regime under which China would prosper, make fresh and significant contributions to civilization and achieve a regime which would be a creative synthesis of its ancient culture with the democratic ideals and institutions of the West, two major menaces stood in the way. One was Communism of the Russian type with its assumption of the word democracy, a word to which it gave an interpretation which in many ways was the exact opposite and in others a distortion of that given in the West. The other was the ambition of a powerful group of elements in the island neighbour, Japan. Eventually these two, first the second and then the first, dealt the Nationalist Government such blows that it was driven off the mainland and was confined to a precarious refuge on Formosa. The full scale invasion of China by Japan which so weakened the Nationalist regime that it was swept off the Continent by the Communists did not begin until July 1937. However, as we have seen, even before the beginning of their triumphant northward advance, the Nationalists had been confronted by both. July 1937 marked the beginning of a decisive stage in the weakening of the Nationalist regime by the Japanese. That stage ended with the defeat of the Japanese in the summer of 1945. There then followed the attempt of the Nationalists to give the populace the internal peace, order, and prosperous reconstruction for which it had been hoping, the triumph of the Communists, and the efforts of the latter to reshape the country according to their ideals. It is these two stages, namely that from July 1937 to August 1945, and that from August 1945 to the time when these lines are being penned, the summer of 1953, which must engage us successively in the next two chapters. In the remaining paragraphs of this chapter we must summarize the relations with Communism and Japan of the Nationalist (Kuomintang) Government after the latter had achieved the ostensible reunion of China in the summer of 1928.

After their failure to win the Kuomintang by co-operating with it and the complete break of the latter with them in the summer of 1927, the Communists were faced with the necessity of a drastic change in leadership and programme. Details are complex and confusing. A bare outline of some of the more important developments may serve as a guide through the maze. In July 1928 what was called the Sixth Congress of the Chinese Communist Party convened in Moscow under the watchful eye of the Kremlin and Stalin. Elements deemed objectionable by Stalin were either prevented from attending or were weeded out. Given important places by the Congress were Li Li-san and Chou En-lai. A little over a year later Ch'ên Tu-hsiu was expelled from the party. In 1931 he and various dissidents met in Shanghai and organized on the advice of Trotsky. In the autumn of 1932 he and some others of the Trotskyites were arrested and imprisoned by the Kuomintang, and he faded out of the scene, so much so that his death in 1942 near Chungking scarcely caused a ripple.

In the meantime Mao Tse-tung came to the fore. In contrast with Li Li-san, who believed that the winning of the country to Communism was to be accomplished by organizing the urban labourers, especially in the modern factories and their related occupations, among them the railway workers, Mao Tse-tung held that it could best be brought about by mobilizing the peasants and inciting them to rise against the landlords. Since China was predominantly agricultural and modern industries were in their infancy and enrolled only a small minority of the population, although it could not easily be reconciled with orthodox Marxism and Stalinism, this procedure seemed to have a better chance of success. Much of the land was owned by those who cultivated it, but enough was rented and sufficient irritation against the proprietors existed to make attractive among many peasants propaganda for the confiscation of the holdings of the landlords and their redistribution among those who tilled the soil. In 1926 and 1928 Mao initiated this programme in his native province, Hunan. There he joined forces with Chu Teh, who had adopted a somewhat similar method, also in Hunan. Chu

Teh, born in Szechwan in 1886 of well-to-do gentry stock, was given the rudiments of the traditional classical education, but went on to acquire a modern military education, held a command in the early armies of the Republic, was among those who fought to unseat Yüan Shih-k'ai when the latter made himself Emperor, in 1923 joined the Kuomintang, in 1924 went to Berlin to study, and there in 1925 became a member of the Communist Party. Returning to China, in 1927 and 1928 he began to display his military genius by organizing a Communist army, chiefly in the countryside in the provinces of Kwangtung, Hunan, and Kiangsi. Both Mao and Chu were acting against the advice of the Chinese Communist Party.

That party, in its meeting in Moscow, while recognizing the importance of the peasants, calling for the expropriation of the holdings of all landlords, and, approving the guerilla activities of Mao, insisted on the leadership of the industrial proletariat in the revolution. Returning from Moscow with these instructions, Li Li-san attempted to carry them out and in this was aided by Chou En-lai. However, he found the industrial proletariat lukewarm and, in spite of the occupation of Changsha, the capital of Hunan, by Communist forces for a few days in the summer of 1930, his procedure was obviously not succeeding.

In the meantime, Mao Tse-tung, Chu Teh, and other leaders built up a Soviet regime in the rural areas in Kiangsi, based upon armed forces and the confiscation of the lands of the landlords and rich peasants. For these latter Communism meant a reign of terror, with executions. It was a foreshadowing of what was to be general in China in the mid-century when the Communists took over the country. Although a civilian, Mao managed to achieve the outstanding position and in November 1931 what was called the Chinese Soviet Republic was established with headquarters in Kiangsi and Mao Tse-tung as chairman and Chu Teh as commander-in-chief of its armies. The previous January, Li Li-san, discredited and displaced by order of the Comintern, after a public 'recantation' of his errors retired to Moscow, ostensibly to study. The Chinese Soviet Republic, with tentacles reaching out from Kiangsi into the neighbouring provinces of Fukien and Anhui and with sympathizers elsewhere in China, was becoming formidable.

Chiang Kai-shek, as head of the Nationalist regime, was quite aware of the menace and took active steps to crush it. These were in part military. Armed expedition after armed expedition was launched against it. Other, more positive measures were initiated to undercut the appeal of the Communists. The New Life Movement was one of them. Efforts at rural reconstruction were undertaken to bring about improvement in the lot of the peasants.

So successful did the Nationalists prove to be that in the autumn of 1934 the Communist forces began the evacuation of Kiangsi and started on a memorable long march of about 6000 miles which brought their remnants and their leaders to the north-west with headquarters at Yenan, in the province of Shensi in the great bend of the Yellow River. That trek is one of the epics of history and gave a discipline which was to harden the Communists and prepare them for future victories. They accomplished it by keeping largely to the mountains where they were less accessible to the Nationalist forces. Before the journey was completed thousands of them perished. Somewhat less than 20,000 survived the march across rugged mountains, swift torrents, and deep valleys. In Yenan they were in a region which already had bands that sided with them and they were less easily reached by the Nationalist armies than in the south.

Before the evacuation of the south by the major Communist leaders had lightened the pressure on the Nationalists in that region and heightened it in the north-west, the Japanese menace had dramatically assumed new and alarming proportions. As we have seen, since their defeat of Russia in 1905 the Japanese had been strongly entrenched in Southern Manchuria in their leasehold in Port Arthur and Dairen, in the railways, and in various economic enterprises. Manchuria was obviously debatable ground. Extensive, with large and only slightly developed resources in field, forest, coal, iron, and water-power, it was desired by the three great nations on its borders, China, Russia, and Japan. In 1931 a kind of condominium existed. China was legally the owner, a position reinforced by a population which was overwhelmingly Chinese by birth or ancestry. Yet not since 1911 had a Central Government of China exercised administrative control. That had been by Chang Tso-lin and was now by his son, Chang Hsüeh-liang. Russia, reorganized by the Communists, had made good the claims inherited from the Tsarist regime both (with the aid of the Allies and the United States after 1917) as against Japanese ambitions and, latterly, against the Chinese. In 1915 the Japanese wrung from an unwilling but weak China the extension of their lease from twenty-five to ninety-nine years. In various ways they were developing their interests in the form of mines and industries. Moreover, Koreans, since 1910 Japanese subjects, were moving by the hundreds of thousands across the Yalu River from their overcrowded land into the comparatively empty Manchuria. The Kwantung Army, through which much of Japanese control in Manchuria was exercised, was in the hands of men who would brook no interference with Japanese interests and were bent on extending them. Japan's population was growing, the arable land of the islands could not produce enough to feed it, and livelihood depended on exchanging the products of the country's growing factories for foodstuffs and raw materials. Manchuria seemed a promising outlet for some of the surplus population. It was even more important as a source of raw materials and as an area for industrial development. Under these circumstances a peaceful condominium was impossible.

The Nationalist Government of China was determined to assume effective control of Manchuria and in so doing irritated both the Russians and the Japanese. We have seen how they were checked by the Russians. The Japanese were more drastic. Friction between them and the Chinese arose over a number of issues. Chang Hsüeh-liang was no more disposed to truckle to the Japanese than his father had been. Moreover, he was more inclined to co-operate with the Nationalist regime. The Nationalists claimed that the lease on Port Arthur and Dairen had expired at the end of twenty-five years, namely in 1923, while the Japanese insisted that the extension to ninety-nine years made in 1915 was binding. The Chinese planned a system of railways in Manchuria to compete with those of the Japanese, and this, the latter claimed, violated agreements between themselves and China made at the end of the Russo-Japanese War. Chinese and Japanese could not reach a common mind on who had the right to levy taxes in the zone of the South Manchuria Railway, on the presence of Japanese railway guards for that line, and on obstacles placed by the Chinese authorities over the purchase or renting of land and houses by Koreans and Japanese. In July 1931 Chinese and Koreans clashed over an irrigation ditch. That summer a Japanese army officer was killed in Manchuria by Chinese soldiers.

To cut the Gordian knot the Kwantung Army struck, and struck suddenly. On the night of 18 September 1931 an explosion was heard on the outskirts of the strategic city of Mukden which the Japanese claimed was caused by a Chinese attempt to blow up the tracks of the Chinese Eastern Railway. The Kwantung Army thereupon rapidly took possession of what the Chinese called the Three Eastern Provinces, those which constituted Manchuria. They were almost unopposed by Chang Hsüeh-liang, for at the time most of his troops were south of the Great Wall. Early in 1932 the Japanese set up in Manchuria a state which they called Manchukuo. They claimed that its creation was the spontaneous action of the populace. At its head they placed the last Emperor of the Ch'ing Dynasty, whom we have called P'u-i and who since 1924, when he had been driven out of Peking by Fêng Yü-hsiang, had been living quietly in the Japanese Concession in Tientsin.

The following year the Japanese overran the adjacent province, Jehol, a part of Inner Mongolia, and incorporated it into Manchukuo. In September 1932 the Japanese formally recognized Manchukuo as independent and signed with it a treaty of alliance for joint defence. In March 1934, P'u-i was declared Emperor of the new state, now called Manchukuo, the Manchu Empire. This show of spontaneous secession from China and of independence deceived no one, probably not even the Japanese or the 'Manchukuoans' themselves. Manchukuo was clearly a puppet and was amply supplied with Japanese 'advisers'. In it, as part of their programme, the Japanese attempted a revival of the Confucian tradition and the Confucian state.

Chinese national sentiment hotly resented this Japanese action. It could not hope to win against Japan on the open field of war. It vented itself in a boycott of Japanese goods, banks, and steamers. Even before the Mukden 'incident' this had been in force. It now became more rigorous. In Shanghai the Japanese authorities demanded that the municipal authorities dissolve the associations engaged in the boycott and to enforce compliance and protect their nationals landed marines. In the fighting which ensued much of the city was destroyed. Japanese gunboats also bombarded Nanking (1 February 1932). Japan was employing the methods to which the Western Powers had earlier resorted in their controversies with the Chinese. It was May 1932 before open hostilities ceased.

In the meantime the rest of the world was not idle. As a member of the League of Nations, China appealed to that body within a few hours after the initial explosion at Mukden and urged the United States, which was not a member of the League, to invoke the Pact of Paris. The League of Nations was in an awkward position. Its major members were in the trough of the depression which began in the United States in 1929 and, preoccupied with their economic problems, were not inclined to apply armed sanctions. Nor was the United States in much better case. Moreover, the British, smarting under the recent Chinese actions against them, were scarcely disposed to pull China's chestnuts out of the fire. Even had the two major Western naval powers in the Western Pacific, Britain and the United States, united in an effort at the armed restraint of Japan, the Washington treaty of 1922 which had prevented them from building adequate naval bases in that region had given Japan such a command of those seas that they probably would become involved in a prolonged and costly war in which the odds would be against them.

Both the League and the United States moved promptly, but in a manner which they hoped would bring to their support the moderate and sober elements in Japan as against the swashbuckling militarists. In this they failed. In January 1932, after trying other expedients, the American Secretary of State, Henry L. Stimson, consciously following precedents set by some of his predecessors, formally notified both China and Japan that the United States could not 'admit the legality of any situation . . . which may impair the treaty rights of the United States or its citizens in China, including those which relate to the sovereignty, the independence, or the territorial and administrative integrity of the Republic of China or . . . the open door policy' and that it did 'not intend to recognize any situation, treaty, or agreement . . . brought about by means contrary to the . . . Pact of Paris . . . to which treaty both Japan and China, as well as the United States, are parties'. Thus, by what came to be known as the Stimson Doctrine, the United States refused to give recognition to Manchukuo. In March 1932 the Assembly of the League of Nations took a similar step. It also helped to bring about a cessation of hostilities in Shanghai and late in May 1932 the Japanese forces were withdrawn from that city. The League sent to Manchuria a commission of inquiry headed by Lord Lytton, which had on it an Italian, an American, a Frenchman, and a German. It reported in the autumn of 1932 recommending a government for Manchuria which, largely autonomous, would respect the sovereignty and administrative integrity of China and the rights of all three of the most interested powers, namely Russia, Japan, and China. In February 1933, but not until after heated debate, the League adopted the report, declared that its members would not recognize Manchukuo, called on Japan to desist from her military measures in China, and directed that the dispute be settled under the supervision of the League.

Japan countered by withdrawing from the League (March 1933). In this, the most severe test to which its machinery had thus far been subjected, the League of Nations proved itself unable to bring into line a recalcitrant power. Nor was any power or group of powers disposed to do so. Japan had, in effect, snapped her fingers at the rest of the world and had received only verbal reprimands. While the League continued for a few more years, it had in reality been dealt a fatal blow. Since through it the peace machinery of the world had proved impotent; the Mukden incident became a major step towards World War II. Yet the League and the United States were so far successful that Manchukuo was given formal recognition by very few governments.

In possession of Manchuria through the fiction of Manchukuo, Japan proceeded to develop the resources of the region and to dovetail its economy with her own. In 1935 she bought out the Russian interest in the Chinese Eastern Railway, thus moving Russia out of what had long been her zone. However, the Utopia of which the militarists had dreamed did not materialize. No large immigration from Japan took place, for Japanese farmers were loath to move to a region of severe winters where competition was keen with Chinese farmers and their lower standard of living. Yet Chinese and Koreans continued to pour into the land and the population skyrocketed.

The Japanese chauvinists who were in control of their country were not content with the control of the Three Eastern Provinces and Jehol. From them as a foothold they advanced their borders eastward into Inner Mongolia and southward into the north-eastern portion of China proper.

They were intent upon dominating all China. They wished to do this with the co-operation of the Chinese, but, in effect, by making all that land into a puppet similar to Manchukuo. In April 1934 Tokyo warned the rest of the world to keep its hands off and openly opposed 'any attempt on the part of China to avail herself of the influence of any other country in order to resist Japan . . . [or] any action taken by China calculated to play one power against another . . . [or] supplying China with war aeroplanes, building aerodromes in China, and detailing military and naval instructors or military advisers to China, or contracting a loan to provide funds for political uses.'

Chinese students seethed with indignation, organized demonstrations against Japan, and formed a country-wide federation of local bodies which bore the name of National Salvation Unions. In November 1931 students moved *en masse* on Nanking, demanding action. Because of this and other factors, in December 1931 Chiang and many of the major men in the government resigned. But the next month he was back in power.

The cooler heads among the Chinese, among them Chiang Kai-shek, knowing the superiority of the Japanese in *matériel*, trained officers, aircraft, and the command of the sea, sought to avoid open war and to build up the nation's strength against the day when its armies might meet the Japanese with some hope of victory.

Part of the necessary preparation was the achievement of internal unity. Here the chief but by no means the only obstacle was the Communists. There were war lords and factions which also were handicaps. In pressing the battle against the Communists Chiang Kai-shek was moved not only by the purpose of national unity but also by the deep distrust and implacable enmity born of his experience with them. He directed against them in their new stronghold in the north-west the armies under the command of Chang Hsüeh-liang, now refugees from their Manchurian homes.

Out of this effort came one of the most startling episodes

of a dramatic century. Chang Hsüeh-liang had his head-quarters in Hsian. He did not push the campaign against the Communists as rapidly as Chiang Kai-shek had hoped. That was partly because the Communists were urging his troops to cease fighting their fellow-Chinese and to join forces with them in ousting the Japanese and so to be able to return to their families in Manchuria. Chiang went to Hsian to attempt to push the campaign. There, in December 1936, he was seized and confined by Chang Hsüeh-liang. For a time his life hung by a thread, but after two weeks of negotiations he was released. Chang Hsüeh-liang voluntarily returned with him to Nanking, and there was tried, convicted, and kept permanently in custody.

However, through the episode Chiang Kai-shek suspended hostilities against the Communists. In the negotiations which followed open fighting ceased and what was called a united front was presented against the Japanese. Yet at best the united front was merely a truce. Friction and distrust continued and permanent peace or co-operation would be impossible if the danger of the common enemy were removed.

In spite of some gains, it was a poorly prepared and still only partly united China which faced what the Japanese intended to be quick and decisive action. China needed time, and time was what the Japanese would not give her. Those who shaped Japan's policies were determined to carry out their purpose in China before she should become strong enough to offer effective resistance. They dreamed of a Far East dominated by Japan. That domination, they declared, would be for the benefit of all, but the Japanese would be clearly masters and the other peoples must co-operate with them by doing their bidding.

CHAPTER SEVEN

THE EXHAUSTING STRUGGLE WITH JAPAN : JULY 1937 TO AUGUST 1945

THE attempt of Japan to bring all China to heel was to be expected. In Japan the radical elements in the army who favoured a more vigorous policy in China were moving towards control. In May 1932 a group of young officers assassinated the Premier and for a brief time held the capital in terror. In their trial they were permitted lengthy harangues in which they denounced what they declared to be the supine policy of the government. In August 1935 the head of the Military Affairs Bureau, a major-general, was murdered by a lieutenant-colonel on much the same grounds. In February 1936 several hundred soldiers, led by captains and lieutenants, seized strategic buildings in Tokyo and killed some of the high officials whom they regarded as responsible for what they declared to be the weakness of the administration and the failure to take a more positive foreign policy. Clearly the drift in Japan was away from any compromise of Japan's position in China. At the same time nationalistic sentiment in China was hardening against Japanese encroachments in the north and demanded more forthright resistance. Tension was rising, and those who realized the military weakness of the country and wished to gain time, even at the cost of concessions, were finding it more and more difficult to stand against the tide.

The full-scale invasion by the Japanese began with what at first looked like a minor incident on the night of July 7th, 1937. At Lukuchiao, a bridge in the vicinity of Peiping (Peking), Chinese and Japanese troops exchanged shots. The Japanese were engaged in manoeuvres where they had no legal right to be, but the Japanese Government regarded the situation as extremely grave. Although the local Chinese authorities punished the officers in charge of the Chinese forces and suppressed anti-Japanese organizations, Japan dispatched large reinforcements to the province. Late in that month the Japanese seized Peiping. They also advanced their lines in Inner Mongolia and in Shansi, the province west of that in which Peiping was situated. Obviously they were intent upon extending their control over much of the north, both Inner Mongolia and the northern tier of the provinces of China proper. Some put forth the plea that it was to forestall possible Russian encroachments.

As had been the case after the Mukden incident of 1931, mobs of infuriated Chinese attacked Japanese in Shanghai and several other cities in the Yangtze Valley, and in self-defence Japanese consulates were closed, Japanese subjects were evacuated from some of the more exposed places, and troops and ships were rushed in to protect Japanese interests.

The Japanese now found themselves under the necessity of either withdrawing completely from China or of attempting to seize control of the entire country. In view of the temper in Japan, the latter was the only possible course. The Japanese did not aspire to a direct administration of China such as they had established in Korea. Rather they sought, as they had in Manchuria, to bring into being a government or governments by Chinese which would be subservient to them or, as they put it, would 'co-operate'.

The National Government had no intention of taking the role desired by the Japanese. It threw its best troops and its air force into the fight to protect the main seat of its strength, the Yangtze Valley in and around Shanghai and Nanking. However, it laboured under severe and possibly fatal disadvantages. Its air force was small and once destroyed could not be replaced from domestic sources. Its armies lacked a sufficient body of trained officers. It was deficient in heavy artillery and in motorized equipment and did not have the industries to manufacture them. In accord with long-standing tradition, which had built defences against invasion overland from the north-west, the Chinese navy was of no consequence and could not hope to dispute Japan's mastery of the sea, so that the Japanese could pour in reinforcements unhindered. They quickly wiped out the small Chinese air force and henceforward could bomb Chinese cities at will. They had sufficient heavy industry to provide their armies with all the needed *matériel*. They possessed a large body of trained officers. The only Chinese hope was to oppose distance to invasion, to draw the invaders inland where their lengthened lines would be subject to guerilla operations, and thus in time to bleed them white and by a war of attrition bring Tokyo to a more reasonable mind.

In November 1937 Shanghai came under the control of the Japanese. The next month the Japanese took Nanking, and their troops perpetrated atrocities which the world, as yet not inured by what was so soon to come elsewhere in World War II, viewed with shocked horror. Chiang Kai-shek and his government moved the capital to Hankow. That, however, was easily accessible to the Japanese by water, rail, and air. Accordingly, after a few months the Nationalist Government set up its headquarters at Chungking, on the Yangtze, in Szechwan. Here the Japanese navy could not hope easily to penetrate, for its route would lie against swift currents through the tortuous gorges cut by the Yangtze in the protecting ranges on its course to the sea. Mountains and the absence of railways and highways offered formidable obstacles to the movement of troops and heavy equipment. It was only by air that it seemed possible to worry Chungking and its defenders.

Now there took place an amazing movement to the west and south-west. Tens of thousands of Chinese migrated from the areas occupied or seriously threatened by the Japanese. Many of them went on foot. Among them were students, teachers, and others of the intelligentsia. They sought refuge chiefly in Szechwan and Yünnan Provinces, but some found haven in Kweichow and Kwangsi Provinces and in the western part of Hunan. Numbers of schools and universities in the Japanese zone went to unoccupied or 'free' China, taking with them faculties, student bodies, and such equipment as they could transport by boat or automobile, and once there they either erected temporary accommodation or utilized temples or other existing structures.

The refugees and the existing populations did not always mix happily, for traditional provincial loyalties and prejudices were strong. Yet, in the face of extraordinarily difficult circumstances, during the earlier years of the war marked progress was made in areas under the National Government in education, in local government, in the inauguration of industries, in the organization of co-operatives, and in the construction of highways which, crude though they were, made possible the use of automobiles. Approaches were made to the non-Chinese tribes in the west, among them some on the Tibetan border, in the effort to bring them within the orbit of Chinese culture. For a time hopes were high of what would be accomplished throughout the country during the days of 'reconstruction' which it was believed would follow the defeat and expulsion of the Japanese.

The Japanese were also optimistic. They pushed their lines forward fairly steadily, at first rapidly and latterly more slowly. In October 1938, after a little more than a year of full-scale invasion, they took Hankow and Canton, thus gaining possession of the chief cities of Central and South China. The following March they captured Nanchang, the capital of Kiangsi Province. Some months later they seized cities south and west of Canton in the effort to close some of the gaps through which supplies from the outer world were reaching the Nationalists. In June 1940 they occupied Ichang, at the down-river end of the Yangtze Gorges, thus drawing nearer to Chungking. By this time they had obtained possession of most of the railways, the lower reaches of the main navigable rivers, and the major seaports. Cutting it off from the Western world and depriving it of the source of much of its revenues, they were slowly strangling the National Government.

Technically Japan was still not at war with China. Its avowed purpose was to eliminate a regime which would not co-operate and give the Chinese the opportunity to set up one which would do so. At first the Japanese tried to persuade one of the more respected war lords, Wu P'ei-fu, to head such a government, but when he proved obdurate they found what they hoped would be a compliant tool in Wang Ching-wei. Wang Ching-wei had been a close friend and supporter of Sun Yat-sen, had shared in bringing about the revolution, was with Sun at his death-bed, and had penned the will which Sun had signed and which had been regarded by the Kuomintang as a sacred trust. He had held high office in the National Government, but he was jealous of Chiang Kai-shek. In agreeing to head a government which would collaborate with the Japanese he may have been moved by a combination of ambition, a conviction that the country's best interests would be served in that fashion, and by confidence in his ability to outwit the Japanese. In March 1940 accordingly there was set up at Nanking, with Wang Ching-wei as its head, what the Japanese loudly proclaimed to be the legitimate government of China under what they declared to be the true Kuomintang. In that fiction several Chinese joined who had been active in the Kuomintang.

With this puppet regime at Nanking Japan entered into treaty relations. On the surface the treaty was one between equals. Japan agreed to respect the sovereignty of China and to relinquish its extraterritorial rights. The two governments were to join in defence against Communism, and to this end Japan engaged to supply troops, especially in the north and in Inner Mongolia, near the Communist stronghold. Nanking formally recognized Manchukuo and signed a treaty with it. But if Wang Ching-wei had hoped to deal with the Japanese as an equal he was bitterly disappointed. He was completely dependent on them and in 1944 he died, disillusioned and frustrated.

Under this puppet regime the Japanese set about the development of the resources of the territory. In this they were extending to China proper what they were already doing in Manchuria. Here they had built railways, were developing industries, and were exploiting mines and forests, so that under Japan Manchuria had become the most highly industrialized area of China and had almost as many miles of railways as were to be found in all the rest of the country. So in much of occupied China companies were set up as joint Japanese-Chinese undertakings. Factories, mines, telegraph, railway and bus lines, dockyards, and banks in Japanese-occupied territory became the property either of Japanese corporations or of corporations in which Japanese were in control. Japanese advisers to the puppet governments multiplied.

The Japanese insisted that the schools in the areas which they controlled be made to serve their ends. That was not surprising, especially since for years students had been volubly anti-Japanese and had engaged in anti-Japanese activities. At Japanese insistence textbooks were revised to inculcate loyalty to the 'co-prosperity sphere' which the islanders professed to be setting up in East Asia, and Japanese was substituted for English as the chief foreign language taught.

Yet resistance to the rule of the Japanese and their puppets continued. This was not only from the Nationalist forces and the Communists but also from guerillas and underground groups. Among the latter were many students. Moreover, the Japanese tended to be overbearing and alienated Chinese who might otherwise have collaborated.

We cannot know if Japan would have eventually succeeded in overcoming Chinese opposition and becoming master of the country had aid not come from the outer world and the Far East been drawn into World War II.

Japan had allied herself with the Axis powers. In 1936 she had entered into an anti-Communist pact with Germany, a pact to which Italy adhered in 1937. The European phase of World War II, which opened in the autumn of 1939, was followed in 1940 by the German occupation of France and the Netherlands, and thus the hold of these powers on their possessions in the Far East became shaky. Moreover, for the time being Britain was left alone to oppose the Nazi menace and might not have the strength to resist an attack on her holdings in the Far East. The temptation was very strong upon Japan to move into Indochina, Indonesia, Hongkong, and Malaya, and perhaps into Burma, Ceylon, and India, and build a 'co-prosperity sphere', a 'new order in East Asia'. In September 1940 she regarded her position as strengthened by a three-power pact of herself, Germany, and Italy, promising total aid to one another for ten years. She believed herself relieved of the chronic danger of attack by Russia when, in April 1941, she signed a neutrality treaty with the U.S.S.R., and especially when, in June 1941, Germany invaded Russia. In September 1940 Japanese troops began the occupation of French Indochina, thus cutting off from Nationalist China the flow of supplies from the outside world over the French railway from the coast to Yünnan.

The Japanese seemed to take special delight in flouting the interests and rights of their former ally, Great Britain, and, especially after the outbreak of war in Europe, the British were in no position to enforce such rights. The Japanese may have found peculiar satisfaction in humiliating the Western power which had had a paramount part in forcing open the doors of China, had formerly enjoyed extraterritorial rights in Japan, and had been a major competitor in the trade and shipping of China. Moreover, in one way and another aid was being given by Britain to the National Government. Through Hongkong, a British possession, imports entering Nationalist China were aiding in the resistance to Japan. The British Government continued its recognition of the Nationalist regime and did not recognize Wang Ching-wei's puppet administration as legitimate. It also advanced credits to Chungking. From time to time anti-Japanese agitators sought to take advantage of the relative security of the British Concession in Tientsin and the International Settlement in Shanghai, the latter predominantly British in its management. Then, too, as the Japanese blockade more and more sealed the ports on the China coast in the effort to cut off assistance to the Nationalists from the outside world, a highway was constructed over difficult terrain from Burma, then a part of the British Empire, to Kunming (Yünnanfu), an important city in unoccupied China, and across it goods were being conveyed which reinforced China's resistance. The Japanese insisted, sometimes with scant courtesy, that anti-Japanese activities be suppressed in the British areas in Tientsin and Shanghai. They roughly handled many British subjects in China, fired on several British vessels in Chinese waters, and in August 1937 bombed and machine-gunned the car of the British Ambassador to China. Moreover, in the regions occupied by them they succeeded in having the moneys collected by the Chinese Customs deposited in the Yokohama Specie Bank instead, as had been customary, of the British-owned Shanghai and Hongkong Banking Corporation. From July 1940 to October of that year, to a very considerable loss of British prestige, they induced the British authorities to close the Burma road, and, to reduce friction, in August 1940 Great Britain withdrew all her troops from China.

It was in her relations with the United States that Japan eventually came to her downfall. Ever since the Russo-Japanese War friction had existed between the two countries. The degree of tension varied but mounted fairly steadily after the beginning of the full-scale invasion of China by Japan, which began in July 1937. After that invasion began the United States co-operated with the League of Nations in the latter's efforts to restrain Japan. On 5 October 1937, the Far Eastern Advisory Committee of the League, on which the United States was represented by a non-voting member, declared Japan to be guilty of violating the Pact of Paris, also known as the Kellogg-Briand Pact, and the nine-power treaty which had been signed in Washington in 1922. That same day President Roosevelt in a public address, without specifically naming Japan, called on the 'peace-loving nations' to oppose the 'violations of treaties', which were 'creating a state of international anarchy', and to quarantine war as they would an epidemic disease. The following day the Assembly of the League adopted the committee's report and the American Secretary of State declared that his government was in general accord with the Assembly's action. Similarly, the United States joined in a conference to which Belgium invited the signatories of the nine-power treaty. Japan did not attend, for she had been insisting that she would not tolerate any interference by a third power in her relations with China. The gathering contented itself with reaffirming the principles of the nine-power treaty, for its major members were too deeply involved in complications nearer home to take more positive measures.

For a time late in the 1930s both the Government of the United States and that of Japan seemed intent upon maintaining friendly relations. The United States encouraged the evacuation of its citizens from China, and when on 12 December 1937, Japanese hotheads used planes to bomb three American commercial vessels and the gunboat *Panay* on the Yangtze near Nanking, Tokyo promptly removed the responsible officer from his command and promised indemnity and respect for the rights of Americans, and Washington declared itself satisfied. The United States also withdrew extra forces which had been sent to Shanghai and Tientsin to protect Americans. Many Japanese hoped that the fact that the trade of Americans with Japan was greater than that with China would deter the United States from hostile action, and contended that in the long run Americans would profit by the new order which they aspired to inaugurate in China.

However, public opinion in the United States was mounting against the Japanese invasion. What was known as the American Committee for Non-participation in Japanese Aggression sought to stop exports to Japan from the United States, especially of scrap-iron and petrol, which were utilized by the Japanese forces against the Chinese. Official action against Japan also stiffened. At the end of 1936, through Japanese initiative, the treaty was terminated which arose from the Washington Conference of 1921–2, limiting naval armaments and the fortification of islands in the Pacific, and in 1939 and 1940, released from these restrictions, the United States began to enlarge its navy. This was only partly with Japan in mind, but it was clearly because of the threat of Japan that the United States con-

structed air and submarine bases in various islands in the
Pacific and enlarged its defences in Alaska, Hawaii, and the
Aleutians. The United States Government did not accord
recognition to the Wang Ching-wei regime but instead extended financial credits to the National Government. In
July 1938 the Department of State of the United States
placed what might be called a 'moral embargo' on the export of planes to Japan, suggesting to American manufacturers that, since they were used to bomb civilian
populations, they should not be sold to that country. In
December 1939 the scope was broadened to include the sale
to Japan of the petrol used in aeroplanes. A year later the
United States, acting within its legal rights, denounced its
commercial treaty with Japan. When six months later, on
26 January 1940, the treaty lapsed, the Government of
the United States was free to place such limitations as it
wished on the commerce of its citizens with Japan. In 1940
the export of an increasing number of commodities, including iron and steel scrap and petroleum products, was prohibited. Although that country was not mentioned and the
mounting need of defence was the ostensible reason, it was
quite clear that the action was in large part directed against
Japan. In July 1941 Chinese and Japanese assets in the
United States were 'frozen', and thus trade with Japan was
made more difficult. In October 1938, in a note to Japan,
the United States Government bluntly declared that equality
of opportunity and the open door had ceased to exist in
Manchuria, and in December 1938 the United States re-
iterated its purpose to stand firmly on its treaty rights and
insisted that 'alterations' could rightfully be made 'only by
orderly processes of negotiation' and not by unilateral action
by Japan. Moreover, the United States declared its disap-
proval of Japanese measures in Indochina and of the closing
of the Burma Road.

In the autumn and early winter of 1941 Japanese-
American relations reached a crisis. In November of that
year Japan set forth conditions on which she would refrain from farther advances in South-Eastern Asia. Among

them was the discontinuance of aid from the United States to Nationalist China. A few days later the United States countered with a note which proposed a non-aggression pact to which Japan, the British Empire, China, the U.S.S.R., Thailand, the Netherlands, and the United States would be signatories, the withdrawal of all Japanese forces from China and Indochina, the recognition by Japan of the Nationalist regime as the legitimate government of China, and the surrender by the United States and Japan of their extraterritorial rights in China. In return the United States offered to enter into a new commercial treaty with Japan which would restore trade between them. To this Japan could not assent without a complete retreat from the course which she had been pursuing since at least September 1931. Accordingly, she refused on 7 December 1941, accusing the United States and Great Britain of blocking her efforts for 'the establishment of a general peace between Japan and China' and of seeking 'to maintain and strengthen' their 'dominant position . . . in China' and 'in other areas in East Asia'. Almost at the moment when this note was being presented to the American Secretary of State, and without warning the Japanese attacked the American fleet in Pearl Harbour in Hawaii and dealt it a blow which they believed would cripple it indefinitely. Simultaneously they bombed Singapore, Guam, and strategic centres in the Philippines, moved forces into Northern Malaya, occupied the International Settlement in Shanghai, and announced that a state of war existed between them and the United States and Great Britain. On the following day Great Britain, the United States, and the Netherlands East Indies declared war on Japan. In this Australia and six Latin American countries quickly followed.

Of the wider geographic reaches of the phases of World War II to which Pearl Harbour was an introduction this is not the place to do more than note their existence and the fact that the struggle in China was part of a larger whole and was profoundly affected by it. Pearl Harbour had precipitated the United States into active belligerency. Its vast potential was scattered over many fronts and its concern for the outcome in Europe was given precedence over its aid to the embattled and hard-pressed Nationalist Government in China. The story includes the rapid Japanese advance in the Western Pacific and South-East Asia – the conquest of the Philippines, Malaya, Singapore, Indonesia, and Burma, the heightened control of Indochina, the alignment of Thailand against the United Nations, and the threat to Australia, India, and Ceylon. It is an amazing record. In it is also embraced the sturdy and able resistance of the British Commonwealth, already engaged in the life and death struggle with Hitler in the West, the brave efforts of the Dutch minority in Indonesia, the slow turn of the tide as growing American naval and air power helped to hold and then to push back the Japanese, the resurgence of Russia against the Nazi armies, and the collapse of Mussolini and then of Hitler, followed by the surrender and occupation of Japan in August 1945.

In this China played a part, significant both for herself and for the rest of the world. One of the most urgent problems which confronted the powers allied against Japan was so to reinforce the Chinese that they would not only continue their resistance but would also be able to stage a successful counter-offensive and drive out the invaders. This was not easy. By the time that Pearl Harbour brought the British Commonwealth and the United States into the war against Japan, the latter was in possession of most of the coast of China and thus was able to prevent aid reaching the Chinese by way of the sea. In the closing days of 1941 and the early months of 1942 Japan had plugged most of the remaining gaps in her blockade. On Christmas Day 1941, she took Hongkong, for nearly a century the main centre of British strength on the China coast. On 15 February 1942, Singapore and its reputedly impregnable naval base were forced to capitulate. A little earlier Japanese planes had sunk two great British battleships. For the time being British naval and land power in the Far East had all but been erased. By the middle of March, Japanese forces, moving in from a compliant Thailand, had taken Rangoon and were advancing rapidly on Mandalay. A few weeks later they had seized the southern terminus of the road leading from Burma to Kunming. The completion of their conquest of Burma seemed effectively to seal that door to unoccupied China. Japanese planes were bombing some of the cities of India and Japanese forces had gained a foothold on the Aleutians and were threatening the mainland of Alaska. The overland routes from Russia were still open, but they were long and difficult and little help could have come from that direction, even if the U.S.S.R. had not been estopped by the neutrality treaty with Japan and by the German invasion. Allied ingenuity and daring created air connexions with India. Chinese and American pilots flew regularly over 'the hump', the lofty and tangled mountain barriers between India and 'free' China, and eventually they brought in each month more than had ever come over the Burma road. However, they were subject to attack by Burma-based Japanese planes and most of their freight was absorbed in building up and supplying American forces in China.

By the close of 1944 it looked as though Japan might succeed in crushing the National Government and with it the major Chinese resistance. This was in spite of the fact that in 1944 Americans were slowly pushing the Japanese back from some of their recently won outposts in the Pacific and were beginning the bombings which in the following year were to lay waste most of Japan's major cities, that British and American air, submarine, and surface sea forces were taking a heavy toll on Japanese shipping, and that Chinese, British, and American armies were expelling the Japanese from northern portions of Burma and re-establishing land communication with Nationalist China.

The reasons of the decline in the strength of the Nationalist regime were varied. One was the exhaustion from the prolonged war, a war which had really begun in September

1931. A symptom of the exhaustion was the mounting inflation. This was due to the spiralling costs of the war and the reduction of revenue through the Japanese seizure of the ports and hence of the customs and to the cutting off of taxes from the sections held by the Japanese and the Communists. Partly as a result of the prolonged strain of the war, dissensions were developing between the various factions in the Kuomintang. Moreover, corruption, never entirely absent, was increasing. Cut off from the commercial and industrial centres of East China, the Kuomintang relied more and more for support on the conservative landlord class in West China. It was timid about basing its strength on the masses or moving in the direction of democracy. Its armies were too large and too poorly equipped and officered.

Then, too, friction developed between the Chinese and the Americans. In the early years of the Japanese attack on China, the sympathy of the Americans was uncritically and emphatically with the latter. Chiang Kai-shek was idealized and lauded as a hero, a paragon, and a champion of democracy. In the 1940's the pendulum swung the other way. Reports of the corruption in the National Government were circulated and magnified. American aid was said to be misappropriated to line the pockets of Chinese officialdom. Reactionary, anti-democratic elements in the Kuomintang caught the attention of American observers, and the National Government was declared to be employing concentration camps and other methods of a police state and a totalitarian 'Nazi' regime to suppress opposition, especially that of liberal, democratic elements. Many Americans cynically declared the denomination of 'free' as applied to the China unoccupied by the Japanese to be a tragic misnomer. As American forces in China increased, numbers among them, both officers and men, were arrogant in their contacts with the Chinese, and here and there were guilty of atrocities. General Stilwell, for a time the head of the American army in China and to whom President Roosevelt had asked Chiang Kai-shek to give command of the Chinese forces as well, held Chiang in vast contempt and the two could not happily co-operate.

The debilitating tension between Americans and Chinese was partly allayed by the cancellation of their extra-territorial privileges by Great Britain and the United States. These chronic sources of irritation were removed by the signing, in 1943, of new commercial treaties between the two Western powers on the one hand and China on the other. That same year the United States repealed the legislation which had excluded Chinese from immigration to to its territories and permitted them to be naturalized. This was also a gesture of good will which removed a long-standing grievance.

We must note, too, that in the territories which they controlled the Japanese were eliminating some of the features of foreign domination. In 1943 they turned over to the Chinese their concessions in five cities, the British concessions in Canton and Tientsin, and the International Settlements in Amoy and Shanghai. Italy, as one of the Axis powers, surrendered her concession in Tientsin, and Vichy France withdrew from her holdings in Canton, Tientsin, and Hankow. Japan also conceded to the Nanking regime the right to tax her citizens and their property, returned to their 'rightful owners' numbers of industrial plants in the Yangtze Valley, and eased travel restrictions and duties. To be sure, all this was within areas which the Japanese occupied and to a regime dominated by them, but it established a precedent from which it would be difficult to depart if China ever became once more fully independent.

Moreover, Great Britain and the United States ostensibly accorded to Nationalist China the position of a major power as a co-belligerent. Late in 1943 Prime Minister Churchill, President Roosevelt, and Generalissimo Chiang Kai-shek met in Cairo and agreed upon the conditions which they would impose on Japan in the event of that country's defeat.

The Japanese gains in China in 1944 were impressive

and for the time seemed ominous. They included the seizure of most of the railroads which had remained in Chinese lands. Especially important were sections of the line from Peking to Canton. Their control gave the Japanese an uninterrupted route from Manchuria to Canton and made them partly independent of the sea. This was the more significant since the Japanese navy, suffering from the inroads of the Allies, could no longer be depended upon to supply the Japanese forces in China. Moreover, American airfields to the east of that line were now cut off from unoccupied China. The Japanese also pushed westward, threatening vital centres on the routes which connected 'free' China with Burma and India. At the end of 1944 the position of the Nationalist regime was extremely grim.

The situation was further complicated by the existence of two governments in unoccupied China, that in Chungking, dominated by Chiang Kai-shek, and the Kuomintang, and that of the Communists with its headquarters in Yenan.

During its Yenan period, which began after the 'long march' from south of the Yangtze after Chiang Kai-shek's forces had made its strongholds there untenable, the Chinese Communist Party grew in strength and developed in organization and programme. The uneasy peace and the ostensible united front with the Kuomintang against the Japanese which arose from the seizure of Chiang Kai-shek by Chang Hsüeh-liang late in 1936 gave the Communists a welcome breathing space.

For a time it looked as though the Kuomintang and the Communists might peaceably co-operate. In February 1937 the Central Committee of the Chinese Communist Party formally told the Central Executive Committee of the Kuomintang that if the nation's strength were directed against external aggression it would place its army under the direct leadership of the Military Affairs Commission of the National Government, make its government a part of that of the Republic of China, and cease expropriating the holdings of the landlords. The Kuomintang and the

Communists seemed to come to substantial agreement and civil war ceased. In September 1937 the Communist Party declared that it would no longer seek to overthrow the Kuomintang by force, that it would strive for the enforcement of Sun Yat-sen's *San Min Chu I*, and that it would abolish its own government and its army. Chiang Kai-shek hailed this as 'the triumph of national sentiment over every other consideration'. In March 1938 the Kuomintang brought into being the People's Political Council for advisory purposes and on it the Kuomintang, the Communists, and various minor parties were represented. Temporarily the agreement seemed to be in process of implementation.

However, by the latter part of 1938 Kuomintang-Communist relations were seriously deteriorating. The Communists set up what was in effect a separate state with a distinct government and its own currency and postal system. Chiang was accused of keeping some of his best troops out of the struggle against Japan and on guard on the border between the Nationalist and Communist territories. The National Government also (1939) began a blockade of the Communist-dominated areas in the northwest. Early in 1941 a Kuomintang army attacked a Communist army in Kiangsi and Fukien which in theory had been reorganized as the New Fourth Army in the united front and so defeated it that its remnants were forced to take refuge in Shantung and the adjacent northern part of the province of Kiangsu.

Attempts at mediation were made, partly through the minor parties in the People's Political Council, and in 1944, as the Japanese threat mounted, discussions between representatives of the Kuomintang and the Communist Party seemed to give some promise of reconciliation.

That year President Roosevelt also took a hand in seeking to bring the two elements together in resistance against Japan. On his behalf Vice-President Wallace went to China in an effort to effect a reconciliation and also to promote better relations between the National

Government and the U.S.S.R. and in the autumn of 1944 General Hurley came to China first as personal representative of President Roosevelt and then as Ambassador. Hurley flew to Chungking by way of Moscow. There Molotov, on behalf of the U.S.S.R., appeared to disavow any support of the Chinese Communists. He declared that they were not really Communists and that his government was not associated with them and was not giving them aid. He said that he would be glad if the United States would help the Chinese unify their country against Japan. In China Hurley sought to bring the National Government and the Communists together. He flew to Yenan and returned to Chungking with a concrete proposal from the Communists for an agreement between themselves and the Nationalists. This the Kuomintang rejected. However, in January 1945, a conference was held in Chungking in which Chou En-lai represented the Communists and three high-ranking officials spoke for the Nationalists. At the invitation of both parties, Hurley was present. But in February 1945 the conference adjourned without having achieved its objective. Chiang Kai-shek deeply distrusted the Communists and was persuaded that they were manoeuvring to obtain full control of the government. The Communists were equally convinced that the Kuomintang was determined to have its own way. Hurley was of the opinion that the Communists were 'not in fact Communists', but were 'striving for democratic principles', that the Kuomintang, far from being Fascist, was also 'striving for democratic principles', and that if the United States were patient it could further a reconciliation. After Hurley left for Washington, the American Chargé d'Affaires advised military assistance from the United States to the Communists as well as that which was already being given the Nationalists and believed that this would promote the desired unity. In April 1945 in a conference which Hurley had with him and Molotov in Moscow, Stalin said that Russia agreed with the United States in its support of the National Government and would co-operate with Great Britain and the United States in the effort to bring about the unification of the armed forces in China. He also affirmed that he regarded Chiang Kai-shek as 'selfless' and a 'patriot'.

Yet Hurley was not deceived into believing that he had succeeded in bringing the Kuomintang and the Communists to an agreement or that Russia would not support the Communists. In a report made to Washington from Chungking in July 1945 he said that while he was of the opinion that the strength of their armed forces and territories had been exaggerated, the Chinese Communists fully expected Stalin to support them rather than the National Government. He declared that if they were right, they could bring about a civil war in China.

In the meantime, as we have suggested, the Communists were consolidating their strength. They carried on a guerilla resistance to the Japanese, but, while this proved remarkably effective, it was in a much more limited area than that which the National Government sought to defend, they engaged in few, if any, pitched battles, and they grew in strength, while the Nationalists, with much wider and heavier burdens, suffered from progressive exhaustion. In contrast with the Nationalists, who distrusted the masses, after their retreat to the west drew their revenues from the landlords and based their strength on them, and hesitated to move in the direction of democracy, the Communists sought to enlist popular support. They did not bear the main brunt of the Japanese attack as did the Nationalists, but employed the war years chiefly in extending their territories, in enlarging the membership and improving the organization of their party, and in recruiting and training an army. It is said that the membership of the Chinese Communist Party rose from 100,000 in 1937 to 1,200,000 in 1945, and that most of this increase was from the peasants. By 1945 it was the largest Communist party outside of Russia. The armed forces of the Communists, also largely from the peasantry, consisted of regular troops, of guerillas who could quickly be transformed into regulars, and of defence corps in towns and villages. These defence corps also became effective instruments for controlling the villages.

In effecting this extension and organization Mao Tse-tung was outstanding and dominant, but he did not achieve this position without struggle. For a time his leading rival was Chang Kuo-t'ao. Chang had early been a member of the Chinese Communist Party and had shared in the 'long march'. In contrast with Mao, who wished for a programme of 'defeat for all', meaning by that the elimination not only of the Japanese but also of the Kuomintang and all other non-Communist elements, Chang advocated 'victory for all', namely, such co-operation with the Kuomintang and other non-Communists that they might be led eventually to conform to the Communist pattern. In contrast with Mao, Chang held that the Soviet form of organization was too alien to Chinese tradition to be feasible. The dispute was referred to Moscow, and Moscow decided in favour of Mao and Chang was expelled from the Party. Some time later, in 1942, what was known as the Cheng-feng Movement confirmed Mao's authority. In it Mao sought to correct what he declared to be the faults of some of the members and thus to tighten the discipline in the Communist Party. He vigorously denounced subjectivism, sectarianism, and formalism, especially in what he called the 'half-intellectuals', who he said had a book knowledge of Marxist-Leninist theory but had not learned how to put it into practice.

Indeed, it was in the field of action that Mao Tse-tung seems to have made his chief and distinctive contribution. In his *New Democracy*, issued early in 1940, he claimed to be making a fresh addition to Marxist-Leninist theory. In fact, however, it contained little that was actually new, but he wrote in a clear, vigorous style which had in it a touch of the old classical excellence and at the same time appealed to the multitude.

A leader who came to the fore in the Yenan period, but in collaboration with Mao Tse-tung, was Liu Shao-ch'i. Younger than Mao but, like him, born in Hunan, the son of a prosperous farmer, and having part of his education in

Changsha, he became an organizer and agitator in the coal mines in the adjacent province and then among the labourers in Shanghai, was for a time in Moscow, and joined in the 'long march'. In some quarters he was esteemed the chief theoretician of the Chinese Communist Party, and in 1943 he became the Secretary of the Central Secretariat of the Party. In general he was regarded as following rather closely the Moscow line.

In Yenan life was simple and austere, both for the rank and file of the Party and their leaders. To be sheltered from Japanese bombing planes advantage was taken of caves in loess cliffs, for the loess soil which characterized the region lent itself to excavation. Here were schools, homes, and offices.

In the areas controlled by them the Communists set about reorganizing the economic and social structure somewhat after the manner which was later to become familiar in most of China. The ideals and programmes of the new order were set forth in *The New Democracy*. This 'new democracy' was to be an intermediate and transitional stage between the colonial and semi-colonial status in which Mao described China as having been and true socialism. Communists confiscated the holdings of the landlords, both those who were local residents and those of absentees, and redistributed them among the peasant-cultivators. They organized rural co-operatives for the better utilization of the land. They educated youth in Communist principles and gave women a larger share in the life of the community than had been customary in Confucian China.

In contrast with the exhausted Kuomintang, the Chinese Communist Party came to the year 1945 with a tightly knit, disciplined membership inured to hardship, with its dissidents either eliminated or safely under control, equipped with armed forces which had been indoctrinated with its convictions, and with a philosophy of history and a programme held with unshakable conviction and missionary fervour. With the possible exception of the Kuomintang it was by all odds the strongest party in China. It was more compact and united than its rival and it had much less of corruption in its ranks.

In mid-1945 the leaders of Japan admitted defeat, and in August of that year they surrendered in the dramatic scene on the battleship *Missouri* in the bay of Tokyo and submitted to occupation, unprecedented in their long history, by the Allied powers. The evacuation from China of their forces and other nationals followed. With it came the problems of administering the areas which they had occupied and of reconstruction of a country bled white and disorganized by the long struggle.

Reconstruction was complicated by the attitude of the victorious powers and by the situation elsewhere in East and South-East Asia, including India, areas which bordered China and whose future would affect that of China.

Of immediate importance were the policies and actions of Great Britain, the United States, and Russia. These were given point by decisions reached through a meeting of Prime Minister Churchill, President Roosevelt, and Marshal Stalin at Yalta, in the Crimea, in February 1945. On 11 February 1945, the three men signed an agreement by which the *status quo* in Outer Mongolia (also described as the Mongolian People's Republic) was to be preserved (and by the latter designation Russia later held that this meant the independence of that country); the southern part of Sakhalin, ceded to Japan in 1905, was to be returned to Russia; Dairen was to be internationalized and the pre-eminent interests of the U.S.S.R. in it were to be recognized; the lease on Port Arthur granted to Russia in 1898 and transferred by her to Japan in 1905 was to be restored to the U.S.S.R.; the Chinese Eastern Railroad and the South Manchurian Railroad, providing an outlet to Dairen, were to be placed under a joint Soviet-Chinese company, and the dominant interests of the U.S.S.R. in the lines were to be safeguarded; and the Kurile Islands were to be handed over to the U.S.S.R. However, the agreement also stipulated that China should retain full sovereignty in Manchuria, that the provisions concerning Outer Mongolia, Dairen, Port Arthur, and the railroads would require the concurrence of General-issimo Chiang Kai-shek, and that the U.S.S.R. stood ready to conclude a pact of friendship and alliance with the National Government of China 'in order to render assistance to China with its armed forces for the purpose of liberating China from the Japanese yoke.'

For some time it had been clear that the U.S.S.R. was intent upon continuing in its own way the eastward expansion of Tsarist Russia and that it would not be content until holdings which the latter had once claimed or possessed, and which had been yielded to Japan, were given it. Presumably the U.S.S.R. would have found some way to effect its ambitions even had Great Britain and the United States not assented. Moreover, when the agreement was signed such information as President Roosevelt had led him to believe that Japan was still so strong and determined that she would hold out for many months and that a direct invasion of her shores, costly in Allied, and especially American lives, would be necessary for her defeat. Then, too, Roosevelt seems to have had less faith in the power of the American navy and air force to bring Japan to her knees than the event proved and to have believed that, if she were to be defeated, it must be primarily on the land by crushing her armies in China, including Manchuria. It seemed to him important, therefore, to induce Russia to depart from its neutrality pact with Japan, a pact which Russia conveniently regarded as violated by Japan through the latter's assistance to Germany, and to come actively into the war to expel Japan from China. Roosevelt's acquiescence was made easier by his conviction that Russia was entitled to the ice-free port in the Far East which would be assured by the control of Dairen and Port Arthur.

The National Government of China made the best of the embarrassing, almost insulting, failure to consult it on issues so closely affecting the independence and territorial integrity for which it had endured such sacrifices. In May 1945 Harry Hopkins, on behalf of President Truman, who had come to that office on the death of President Roosevelt a few weeks earlier, went to Moscow. Marshal Stalin assured him that he proposed no alteration in sovereignty in Manchuria or any other part of China, that the Soviet system was not in existence in Mongolia, that Chiang Kai-shek was the only Chinese able to undertake the unification of China, that the Chinese Communists were not as nearly qualified for it, that, since Russia was to be preoccupied with its own reconstruction after the German invasion, the reconstruction of China would have to depend upon assistance from the United States, and that he would welcome Chinese civilian participation in taking over the administration of Manchuria. On 4 June 1945, Truman told T. V. Soong brother-in-law of Chiang Kai-shek and Premier and Foreign Minister of China, what Stalin had said. The following day Hurley, still American Ambassador to China, disclosed to Chiang Kai-shek the provisions of the Yalta agreement and Stalin's oral assurances of Chinese sovereignty in Manchuria and concurrence in the principle of the open door in China. In July and August T. V. Soong and another representative of China entered into prolonged negotiations in Moscow. At first Russia seemed intent upon obtaining more than had been promised at Yalta. However, partly because of the attitude of the American Ambassador in Moscow, in the resulting treaty and exchange of notes Russia agreed to modifications which were slightly in China's favour.

The terms of the treaty and agreements entered into between the Republic of China and the U.S.S.R. on 14 August 1945, can be briefly summarized. First there was a treaty of friendship and alliance. By it the two governments promised 'to collaborate in the common war against Japan until her unconditional surrender...not to enter into separate negotiations with Japan and not to conclude, without mutual consent, any armistice, or peace treaty either with the present Japanese Government or with any other government or authority set up in Japan which do[es] not renounce all aggressive intentions...not to conclude any alliance and not to take part in any coalition directed against the other ...to work together in close and friendly collaboration after the coming of peace, and to act according to the principles of mutual respect for their sovereignty and territorial integrity and of non-interference in the internal affairs of the other.' The treaty was to remain in force for thirty years. By an exchange of notes the U.S.S.R. 'reaffirmed its respect for China's full sovereignty over the Three Eastern Provinces [namely, Manchuria] and recognize[d] their territorial and administrative integrity.' China agreed to the independence of Outer Mongolia if a plebiscite in that country demonstrated the desire of its people for that status, declared Dairen a free port open to the commerce and shipping of all nations, promised to lease wharfs and warehouses in Dairen to the U.S.S.R., to exempt from customs duties goods passing through Dairen to and from Soviet territory, agreed to the joint use by the U.S.S.R. and herself of Port Arthur as a naval base under a commission of which two members were to be appointed by China and three by Russia and with a Russian as chairman, and assented to the defence of Port Arthur by Russia. In respect to military operations in Manchuria for the expulsion of the Japanese, China and Russia agreed that the prosecution of the war should be under the Commander-in-Chief of the Soviet forces, but that as soon as military operations had ceased in any section the Chinese National Government was to 'assume full authority in the direction of public affairs' and was to 'render the Commander-in-Chief of the Soviet forces every assistance and support through its civil and military authorities.' As to the Chinese Eastern and South Manchurian Railways, they were to be united, their ownership was to be divided equally between Russia and China, they were to be under a board of directors of whom five were to be appointed by China and five by Russia and with a Chinese as president and a Russian as vice-president, their manager was to be a Soviet citizen and their assistant manager a Chinese, the Chinese were to assume responsibility for the protection of the railway, and they were to secure a supply of coal for the railway.

It was under this treaty and these agreements that Russia poured troops into Manchuria.

CHAPTER EIGHT

THE SEIZURE AND REMAKING OF CHINA
BY THE COMMUNISTS

THE defeat of Japan in the summer of 1945 was at an earlier date than many, including President Roosevelt, had anticipated. It confronted the Chinese with the problems of disarming and repatriating the Japanese occupying armies, the re-occupation and administration of the areas won by the Japanese, the reconstruction of devastated areas, the repair of disrupted and impoverished transportation systems, especially railways, the relief of famine, the raising of the standard of living, better public health measures, improved medical care, the achievement of a balanced budget and a stable currency, progress towards the democratization of the country, and national unity.

Each of these was formidable and would have taxed the strength of the strongest government. Some had been present before the Japanese invasion and all had been aggravated by that catastrophe. For instance, transportation in China had long been backward when compared with that of other civilized countries, poverty had been chronic and famines had again and again been precipitated by floods and droughts, population was pressing hard on subsistence and seems to have mounted during the preceding decades, for decades currency had been a problem, and democracy such as was known in Great Britain, Canada, Australia, New Zealand, and the United States was far from being achieved. Moreover, not since the collapse of the Ch'ing Dynasty had all the country been under one administration. In one way or another Manchuria had been separately administered, and the National Government under the Kuomintang was confronted by another and hostile government, that of the Communists.

The solution of these problems would brook no delay. Millions had been buoyed up during the long, agonizing resistance to Japan by a utopian hope of rapid reconstruction and advance once the enemy was defeated and expelled. They would hold accountable any regime which failed to make rapid and substantial progress towards that goal.

It was upon the National Government of the Kuomintang with Chiang Kai-shek as its outstanding figure that the burden of these problems initially fell. It was the regime recognized by the Allies. In theory it was one of the major powers, the others being Great Britain, the United States, and the U.S.S.R., which had brought Germany, Italy, Japan, and their collaborators to their knees. When, in the spring of 1945, the United Nations was formed, China, and by that was meant the National Government, was given one of the five permanent seats on the Security Council of that body, the others being the United Kingdom, France, the U.S.S.R., and the United States.

Yet the National Government was tragically weak. As we have seen, until the Japanese invasion it had been gaining strength and seemed on the way towards achieving the full union of the country and a progressive synthesis of what had been inherited from the old China with the liberal democracy of the Occident. The succession of blows dealt it by Japan had drained its strength. When in 1945 it was suddenly confronted by the gigantic problems thrust on it by the surrender of Japan, it was suffering from corruption, near-exhaustion, and division among internal factions. Of its allies, only the United States and the U.S.S.R. were in a position to render it substantial assistance. The latter, as we are to see, soon turned against it and shifted its support to the Chinese Communists and to the regime set up by them. The former gave aid, but whether through ineptness or perplexed irresolution or because no assistance from without could have salvaged the situation, it failed to prevent the debacle. Within a little over four years after the defeat of Japan, the National Government was driven out of China and was probably saved from being expelled from its last foothold, Formosa, only by the navy of the United States.

It was the Chinese Communists who took over the country. For this, by a strange irony, Japan was chiefly responsible. A major reason for Japan's invasion of China had been antagonism towards Communism and the traditional fear of Russia. By weakening the National Government of the Kuomintang, Japan had made possible the triumph of Communism and the close alliance of the Communist regime with Russia.

The victory of Communism was more than the defeat of the National Government, the Kuomintang, and Japan. It was a breath-taking fulfilment of more than the rosiest dreams of the Russian imperialists of 400 years, the extension of Russian influence over all the mainland of the Chinese Empire and the largest block of population on the globe and the close co-ordination of that Empire with Russian purposes and programmes. Moreover, it entailed a gigantic effort at the mass conversion of China and its out-lying dependencies to Communism of the Lenin-Stalin brand. As essential corollaries this involved the eradication of Confucian ideals and ethics, of religious, social, and economic patterns inherited from pre-Communist China, and of what had been coming in from Western Europe, Britain, and the United States. In the numbers of people involved, it was a drastic revolution on a larger scale than mankind had ever seen. Yet it was merely a stage in the revolution brought to China by the impact of the West which had begun decades earlier.

It is to the main outlines of this story that we must now turn. When, in 1953, these lines were penned, the revolution wrought by Communism seemed to be only in its early phases. What the outcome would be no one could foresee. So far as the scroll had been unrolled it was of a scene unprecedented in China's history and of a social experiment which for magnitude was without parallel anywhere on the globe.

In August 1945, as we have suggested, the National Government of China faced an appalling array of problems. They had to be met simultaneously; they could not be dealt with successively. For the sake of clarity we must speak of them one by one, remembering always that in doing so we are giving them a deceptive appearance of simplicity.

The disarming and repatriation of the Japanese was an immediate obligation. Much of this was accomplished fairly promptly, especially since, contrary to what many had expected, in general the Japanese were docile and did not seek to act independently of their government and to maintain resistance after it had surrendered. In this phase of the postwar settlement some aid was given by the Americans. By the end of 1946 about 3,000,000 Japanese – military and civilians – were returned to Japan.

Obviously another of the first imperatives was the reoccupation of the territories which had been under the Japanese. Here the natural ambition was to bring all China under one administration. To stop short of this goal would mean a divided country, and the strong nationalistic sentiment which characterized the intelligentsia would not rest until unity had been achieved. Moreover, the alternative to unity would probably be, as it had been during the war, one area ruled by the Communists and another under the Nationalists. This would almost certainly entail civil strife, for each would seek to eliminate the other. Exhausted by prolonged domestic wars and foreign invasion, the masses were unutterably weary. The country needed nothing so much as a period of peace.

The National Government moved promptly to accomplish the unity of the country, and in doing so was guilty of blunders, several of them serious. It once more set up its capital at Nanking, but some of its officials, returning to East China from their exile in the West, treated their fellow-countrymen who had remained there under the Japanese as traitorous collaborators and aroused their opposition. The first regime given Formosa was singularly corrupt and battened off the island instead of helping it to recover from the damage wrought in the course of the operations against the Japanese. Although the bulk of the population was Chinese by blood and language, it had been there for several generations, since 1895 had been under the Japanese, and viewed the Chinese from the mainland as aliens.

In Manchuria the situation proved especially difficult. As we have seen, not since the revolution of 1911–12 had a central government in China been able to exercise effective control over that region. First the war lord Chang Tso-lin and then his son, Chang Hsüeh-liang, had ruled it almost as though it were an independent country. Chang Hsüeh-liang had been more inclined than had his father to co-operate with the National Government, but in 1931 he had been driven out by the Japanese and the region had become part of the puppet Manchukuo. Although overwhelmingly Chinese in population and culture, its administrative integration with the rest of the country would be no easy task. Complications developed from the presence of the Russians. After its entrance into the war against Japan, the U.S.S.R. sent large bodies of troops into Manchuria, ostensibly to deal with the Kwantung Army of that power. However, it systematically stripped the region of much of its machinery, sending the loot into its own territories. It thus crippled the mines and factories of the most highly industrialized area of China, upon which the Nationalists had counted for aid in reconstruction. The National Government was able to place troops in some of the chief cities, notably Mukden. In this it was assisted by the Russians. It was at the request of the National Government that the Russians delayed their evacuation of Mukden from December 1945 to March of the following year, and the Nationalist forces entered one day after the Russian troops withdrew.

The Communists also moved into Manchuria, at first chiefly occupying the countryside. When the Russians had completed the disarming of the Japanese, taking thousands into captivity, they withdrew the bulk of their forces, but as they did so, whether from deliberate intent or not is debatable, they left large quantities of Japanese guns and ammunition in such fashion that these fell into the hands of the Communists.

Nevertheless, by the year 1947 most of the main centres which had been in the hands of the Japanese were in the possession of the National Government.

When it came to the immediate relief of physical suffering in the areas which it controlled, the National Government was too impoverished and too honeycombed with corruption and inefficiency to deal adequately with the gargantuan demands. Aid came from other countries, some through official and some through private channels. Much was through UNRRA (the United Nations Relief and Rehabilitation Administration). Difficulties were encountered in bringing it to bear upon the areas of need. Moreover, the Communists complained bitterly and loudly that relief went primarily to territories under the National Government and not proportionately to areas under their own rule.

For the same reasons which handicapped efforts at relief, the National Government was slow in rehabilitating the transportation facilities upon which the political unity and economic recovery and prosperity of the country depended. Railways, for example, were in a sad state of disrepair. Here also assistance came from abroad, largely but by no means entirely through various agencies of the United States Government. Here, too, the disorganization in China was such that there were delays in applying what was made available. Moreover, some of the American aid was through machines and methods entirely unsuitable to the Chinese *milieu*.

A major problem was the nature and structure of the National Government. As it had been since the 1920's, so in 1945 it was dominated by the Kuomintang, with Chiang Kai-shek as virtual dictator. Could it be made genuinely democratic in the sense in which the Western world understood that term? Could it include representatives of the other parties, most of them small minorities composed largely of intellectuals? But the Chinese Communist Party, while a minority, was not small. It was intent on dominating the country and between it and the Kuomintang were deep distrust and long-standing animosity. At the time there were those who believed that no regime could be devised in which the Kuomintang and the Communists would work together peaceably after the patterns of bi-party or multi-party governments such as were known in Europe, the British Commonwealth, and the United States. From the view-point of the outcome it is clear that they were right. However, in the months which immediately followed the surrender of Japan there were many, both foreigners and Chinese, who hoped and strove for what proved to be the impossible.

The Government of the United States was especially active in attempts to promote internal peace in China by bringing the various parties, particularly the Kuomintang and the Communists, into co-operation through procedures which it regarded as democratic. In November 1945 General Hurley resigned his post as American Ambassador in a letter to President Truman in which he accused career men in the American foreign service in China and in the Department of State of siding with the Communists and of advising the latter not to consent to the unification of their army with the National army unless they were in control. That same month Wedemeyer, American Commanding General in the China theatre, reported to Washington that Chiang Kai-shek would be unable to consolidate his authority in North China without first securing a satisfactory settlement with the Communists, the assistance of foreign administrators and technicians, and 'political, economic, and social reforms through honest, competent civilian officials.' Wedemeyer also maintained that Chiang could not 'occupy Manchuria for many years unless satisfactory agreements were reached with Russia and the Chinese Communists.' Since he believed that an understanding could not be achieved between the Communists and the National Government, he recommended that the United States, Great Britain, and Russia undertake a trusteeship over Manchuria until such time as the National Government had become sufficiently strong to assume control.

In a major effort to bring the Chinese together and thus give the country much-needed internal peace, late in 1945 President Truman sent to China General George C. Marshall as his personal representative and Ambassador. His distinguished record in World War II as Chief of Staff and his previous experience in China seemed to give Marshall unusual qualifications for his task of bringing the influence of the United States to bear for the early 'unification of China by peaceful, democratic methods', and for a brief time it appeared that he might succeed.

In January 1946 he induced the National Government and the Communists to agree to a cessation of hostilities and to set up headquarters in Peiping on which these two and the United States were represented to see that what had been promised was carried out. The Communists even consented to the movement of troops of the National Government into Manchuria to restore Chinese sovereignty. That same month they convened in Chungking a Political Consultative Conference on which the Kuomintang, the Communist Party, and some of the other parties were represented. To it Chiang Kai-shek announced that the National Government would immediately grant certain fundamental democratic rights. He also promised that its findings which looked in that direction would be carried out. In February 1946 the National Government and the Chinese Communist Party agreed to a major reduction of their respective armed forces and their integration into armies which would combine contingents from both and which would be divorced from politics.

In spite of this hopeful beginning the efforts at reconciliation and peace were wrecked by opposition both from within the Kuomintang and the Communist Party. In April fighting between the two armies broke out in Manchuria. In June, 1946, Marshall succeeded in bringing about a truce. However, Communist propaganda vigorously denounced the Americans for alleged favouritism to the National Government and for the presence of American marines in China. In spite of the efforts of Marshall and Dr J. Leighton Stuart, the newly appointed American Ambassador to China and a distinguished missionary educator with long experience in the country, Kuomintang-Communist negotiations foundered and hostilities were resumed. Marshall refused to continue as mediator, giving as the reason for the failure of his mission the deep-seated distrust between reactionaries in the National Government and the Communists, and in January 1947 President Truman recalled him to Washington.

The efforts of the United States Government to bring about internal peace and stability in China did not cease with Marshall's return to Washington. Marshall became Secretary of State and in that office continued his deep concern for China. Ambassador Stuart, with his extensive and intimate knowledge of the country and its leaders, was unflagging in urging upon the Chinese remedial measures. In the summer of 1947 President Truman sent General Wedemeyer on a fact-finding mission. On leaving China after his tour of investigation Wedemeyer spoke out bluntly on what he deemed the mistaken military policy and the corruption and inefficiency of the National Government. Because of the drain of the continued fighting in Manchuria, he recommended to President Truman that the United Nations take immediate action to bring about a cessation of hostilities there and that the region be put under a guardianship with China, Russia, Great Britain, France, and the United States as trustees. He feared that the alternative would be Communist domination of Manchuria and ultimately of all China.

From time to time after the defeat of Japan the United States continued to give substantial assistance to the National Government. This was in a variety of ways, some of which we have already noted. It was partly through transporting troops to take over regions evacuated by the Japanese, partly in assisting in the repatriation of Japanese, partly in relief, some of which went through UNRRA, partly in military supplies, and partly in credits.

Since the several and prolonged efforts of the United States Government did not prevent the collapse of the

National Government and the triumph of the Communists, there was much soul-searching in the United States to ascertain the causes of the defeat, especially since it was the worst reverse in foreign affairs which that nation had experienced. Critics of the Democratic administration then in power were especially vocal. They attacked the Yalta agreements, they claimed that insufficient aid had been accorded the National Government, that assistance had been withheld at critical times, and that the cease-fire which Marshall had brought about had given the Communists a breathing-spell when the Nationalists were gaining against them and had enabled them to recoup and enlarge their forces. Whether, had the United States adopted other policies, the outcome would have been altered would probably be debated for many years. Basic, however, as we have more than once said, was the exhaustion of the National Government brought by the Japanese invasion and the long resistance to the enemy. It is extremely doubtful whether assistance from any foreign power or group of powers could have substantially altered the outcome unless the U.S.S.R. had co-operated cordially – and that it was not disposed to do.

Some attempts were made by Chiang Kai-shek and the National Government to remedy the situation, in part by seeking to give a broader popular basis for the regime. In November 1946, on the eve of Marshall's departure from China, a National Assembly convened in Nanking with the announced purpose of adopting a new constitution. The Communists and most of the third parties refused to come, and three-fourths of the members were from the Kuomintang, but in spite of the absence of most of the other elements the expectation was officially cherished that the period of tutelage under one party was about to end and that the consummation of Sun Yat-sen's programme in a democratic multi-party regime was soon to be realized. In March 1948 the National Assembly which had been chosen under the new constitution met in Nanking. It was an unwieldy body and its major achievement was the choice of a President of the Republic. After an initial refusal, Chiang

Kai-shek was elected to the office. Contrary to Chiang's wishes, Li Tsung-jen, who had first come to prominence as a war lord in Kwangsi but had long co-operated with the National Government, was made Vice-President.

The prestige of the National Government rapidly fell. Internal dissensions, corruption, and failure to bring peace and the longed-for reconstruction led many to the conclusion that any regime would be better. Numbers of the intelligentsia, and especially of the students, were alienated by the measures taken to repress dissent, measures which were clearly those of a police state. Public confidence was further shaken by the failure of what had been loudly trumpeted as the end of inflation. In the summer of 1948 a new currency was issued ostensibly based on gold. To acquire the requisite reserves the government ordered that there be surrendered to it all the silver, gold, and foreign currency held by individuals. Much that had been hoarded was turned in, but revenues still were far from meeting expenses and before many weeks the new currency proved as unreliable as the old. This cost the National Government whatever faith in it remained among the more substantial elements in the country. To them and to the majority of the articulate that government had clearly 'lost the mandate of Heaven'. Like the dynasties which had preceded it, its day was adjudged to be irrevocably past. Public opinion was speaking.

Military disaster after military disaster quickly sealed the doom of Chiang Kai-shek's regime. Since 1946 the tide had been moving against it. At that time the Nationalist forces had held most of the main cities and railroads of the north and seemed to be gaining in Manchuria. They outnumbered the Communist armies and were better equipped. Then they began to lose ground. In 1948 the Communists took Mukden and with it the key to Manchuria. The following January they became masters of Peiping and Tientsin. That April they moved into Nanking, and the next month they occupied Shanghai. In the summer (1949) Hankow, Wuchang, and Hanyang fell to them, and so the heart of the Yangtze Valley was in their hands. That autumn the

Nationalists lost Canton and much of the north-west and Sinkiang. They moved their capital to Chungking, but before the middle of 1950 they had been forced to evacuate not only that city but also their remaining strongholds both on the mainland and in the island of Hainan. Thereupon they moved their headquarters to Formosa. That and a few smaller neighbouring islands were all which remained to them, and the Communists were assembling forces to expel them from that last refuge when, as we shall see in a moment, developments connected with Korea brought the United States as a shield between them and their adversaries. In January 1949 Chiang Kai-shek retired from the Presidency of the National Government. However, he retained his position as head of the Kuomintang, and on March 1st, 1950, he resumed the Presidency. In Formosa he was the rallying centre and dictator of the Nationalist resistance.

The suddenness of the military collapse of the National Government seems to have surprised even the Communists. Few in the swollen Nationalist armies had any stomach for fighting. They had no cause which aroused their enthusiasm. Several contingents, with their commanders, went over bodily to the Communists. Some of the armies were poorly equipped, but representatives of the United States declared that the Nationalists could not lay the loss of even one battle to the lack of arms and ammunition. These had been supplied by the Americans, and some of the later Communist victories had been won by American equipment taken from the Nationalists. In contrast, the core of the Communist army was well disciplined, thoroughly indoctrinated with Communist convictions, and led by officers who lived and dressed as simply as the rank and file.

The Communist triumph could be ascribed in part to the divisions, weakness, corruption, and loss of morale in the National Government, in no small degree due to having borne the brunt of the prolonged Japanese invasion, but the Communist victory must also be attributed to the loss of the support of public opinion and to the lack of any other alternative to the National Government. The only viable choice for the country was between the Kuomintang and the Communist Party. No war lord was strong enough to essay the task of a unified national government unsupported by a party, and, aside from these two, no party or group of parties had a sufficient following to make a successful bid for power. The strength of the Communists was found in the combination of their ideology, held with conviction, the tight organization and discipline of the Party, the army, the tireless devotion and austerity of the leaders, the absence of corruption in Communist officialdom, the appeal to the peasantry, and skill in propaganda.

As the Communists expanded their territories they brought into being several organizations. Among those formed in the fore part of 1949 were the All-China Students' Federation, the All-China Federation of Democratic Women, and the All-China Federation of Democratic Youth. Headquarters of these and of other national Communist organizations were set up in Peiping, to which the old name Peking ('Northern Capital') was now restored. Late in August 1949 the North-East People's Government was formed, and in September 1949 a People's Political Conference convened in Peking and adopted its own Organic Law and the Organic Law of the Central People's Government.

On 1 October 1949, the People's Republic of China was proclaimed, with Mao Tse-tung as chairman and with six vice-chairmen, among them Chu Teh, Liu Shao-ch'i, the Soong sister who was the widow of Sun Yat-sen, and Li Chi-shen. Chou En-lai was Premier of the State Administrative Council and Minister of Foreign Affairs.

As the Communist forces swept forward they claimed to be 'liberating' the cities and areas which they occupied. In contrast with most of the other armies with which China had had experience since the Revolution of 1911, the first wave of Communist troops which effected 'liberation' was orderly, neither looted civilians nor misused women, treated the populace with courtesy, and seemed by its practice to substantiate the claim of the Communists that they were genuinely concerned for the welfare of the people. Communists taught the masses, and especially youth, dances and songs which furthered a contagious enthusiastic conviction that a new age was dawning in which the poverty, civil war, and exploitation by foreigners which had dogged China's past would be no more, and that the rule of the people had arrived.

Whatever may have been its real attitude towards the Chinese Communists when Molotov told Hurley that they were not actually Communists and that his government was not supporting them, and when Stalin assured Hurley that he would co-operate in the support of the National Government, and in spite of its solemn promises to that government in 1945, the U.S.S.R. was prompt to recognize the People's Republic of China. This it did on the very day (1 October 1949) when that regime was proclaimed, and in this it was promptly followed by its satellite countries in Eastern Europe. The Sino-Soviet Friendship Association, which was organized in July 1949, quickly organized branches in the larger cities. Portraits of Mao Tse-tung and Stalin were widely displayed side by side.

In September 1949 the representative of the National Government in the United Nations asked that body to condemn the U.S.S.R. for what it called violations by Russia of the treaty of friendship and alliance of August 1945 and urged its fellow members not to recognize the People's Republic. The United Nations did not take the desired action, but the National Government continued in the United Nations as the Chinese regime recognized by that body.

A few months later, on February 12th, 1950, after negotiations in Moscow which continued over a number of weeks, the U.S.S.R. and the People's Republic of China announced the signing of a treaty for mutual aid. By its terms, in case Japan were to undertake aggression on Russia or China, either alone or in alliance with another power, the other was to come to the aid of the one attacked.

The U.S.S.R. and the Chinese People's Republic were to co-operate on all international questions which seriously affected their mutual interests. They were to respect each other's sovereignty and territorial integrity and neither was to interfere in the internal affairs of the other. The treaty was to run for thirty years and if not abrogated by one or the other with a year's notice it was to hold for an additional five years. By agreement made at the same time, the U.S.S.R. promised to withdraw its forces from Port Arthur and to return the Changchun Railway in Manchuria without compensation when a peace treaty with Japan had been signed or at the latest by the end of 1952, and conceded that the administration of Dairen belonged exclusively to the People's Republic of China. The U.S.S.R. also agreed to aid China with credits of $60,000,000 for five years for the purchase of equipment and other materials in Russia. China was to make repayment in raw materials, tea, gold, and American dollars.

Since, in 1952, it became clear that a peace treaty between the Communist Government of China and Japan was not to be signed by the end of that year (although one between Japan and the National Government refugeeing on Formosa had been negotiated), in September 1952 through an exchange of notes, at the formal request of the Peking regime Russian military units continued at Port Arthur. However, on 1 January 1953, according to schedule, the People's Republic of China resumed the exclusive management of the Changchun Railway.

Late in March 1953 Communist China and the U.S.S.R. signed an additional trade protocol by which the latter was to assist the former in developing industries and mining and was to receive in return certain specified metals and agricultural products, among them the long-standing staple in Russian-Chinese commerce, tea.

How far the alliance between the People's Republic of China and the U.S.S.R. was more than ostensibly one between equals and to what degree, if any, China was now a puppet of Russia was not entirely clear to the outer world. Russian influence in China was certainly greater than it had ever been. As Mao Tse-tung frankly said, the masters of China were 'leaning to the left' in the world scene. They had openly espoused the Marx-Lenin-Stalin ideology and were zealously imposing it on the Chinese. Russian became the major foreign language taught in the schools, supplanting the Japanese recently insisted upon by the islanders in the areas which they controlled and the much more widely used English. Hundreds and perhaps thousands of advisers and technicians were employed in the remaking and reconstruction of the country. By all the devices of high-powered propaganda the U.S.S.R. was presented to the Chinese people as their friend. The country was flooded with printed materials from Russia extolling Communism and berating capitalism and especially the United States as the arch-champion of capitalism. In the 'cold war' between the Russian bloc and the free world Communist China was emphatically on the side of Russia. As we are to see in a moment, arms and planes from the U.S.S.R. enabled the Chinese to persist in their intervention in the Korean war. Russian representatives in the United Nations volubly and vigorously pressed the claims of the Chinese Communist Government. It appeared that by the Communist victory in China Russia was now master of the heart-land of Eurasia, the largest land mass on the globe, and had made an enormous advance in its bid for the mastery of the world.

Yet there were indications that not all the Chinese were tamely subservient to the Russians. Much of public opinion looked upon the invasion of Russian personnel with dislike and disdain. At times in his past, as we have hinted, Mao Tse-tung had not hesitated to depart from instructions from Moscow and to devise and follow a policy of his own, and in this he had carried the Party with him. The Chinese Communists had been so successful in achieving the mastery of the country, were so denunciatory of the former infringements on Chinese sovereignty by non-Communist foreign powers, and were dealing so arrogantly with them and their citizens, that it was unlikely that they would submit to dictation from the Kremlin. Presumably most of the leaders of the Chinese Communists regarded the China under their control as an equal partner in the alliance, one which not only needed Russia but which Russia also needed. The prolonged negotiations which preceded the major agreements were interpreted in some circles in the outer world as betokening difficulty and friction in arriving at the published conclusions. The death of Stalin early in 1953 removed an outstanding figure who, in Communist China, stood for the greatness of the U.S.S.R. It seemed unlikely that any living Russian would be as revered in China as had he. Moreover, resentment against Russia and what looked like its control was rising. Like most international alliances, the marriage was one of convenience. But, at least in 1953 when these lines were penned, there seemed to be no indication that Communist China would soon go the way of Communist Yugoslavia and break with Moscow.

Internally the Communists gave China the strongest government which that land had known since the days of the great Manchu Emperors of the seventeenth and eighteenth centuries. Some observers would go further and call it the strongest that the Chinese had ever had.

Certainly the Communists set about the thorough remaking of the Chinese people and their culture. In the four years of their mastery which followed the expulsion of the Nationalists and which, because of the date when it was written, is all that this survey can compass, they had swept away more of the inherited culture of the land and had carried the population further from its ancient moorings than had been done in all the previous half century and more of the revolution brought by the coming of the West. The Communists attempted to inculcate in all Chinese their ideology with its view of the universe, man, history, ethics, and the structure of society. While theoretically endorsing 'freedom of religion', they viewed religion as 'the opiate of the people' and would curb it wherever and whenever it opposed the new order into which they were seeking to bring China. They insisted that Christians cut off all connexion with their brethren in the West. For Roman Catholics this would entail severing the tie with Rome. For Protestants it meant the 'three self' movement – namely, financial self-support, self-government (independence of any direction by foreigners), and self-propagation of the faith. For both Roman Catholics and Protestants it involved the removal of foreign missionaries. The majority of missionaries were permitted to depart after making application for permission to do so. A minority were detained, imprisoned, and tried on various grounds, chief among them being the charge that they were spies and agents of imperialistic governments which were hostile to Communism and China. Then, often after a mass meeting in which the authorities sought to discredit them with the public, they were expelled. A few died in prison. By the middle of 1953 China had fewer foreign Christian missionaries than at any time in a hundred years. Yet in 1953 Christianity was still strong and was, with the possible exception of Islam, the most vigorous of the religions in China. Citizens of western countries other than missionaries were also withdrawing or being expelled. For Buddhism and Taoism the programme involved the expropriation of many temples and monasteries and their lands and an attitude which regarded the monks as parasitic drones who must be constrained to take up occupations of use to the people. The remnants of Confucianism were viewed as a major enemy. Efforts were made to break up the traditional family and its Confucian ethics. Children were taught to denounce their parents as reactionaries. Women were given a larger place in public life. The way of 'the mean' with its distrust of extremes which had been a feature of Confucianism was contradicted. Confucian society was condemned as feudal. Thus what had long been the foundation of Chinese society and culture was being further weakened.

Yet the Communists were endeavouring to rally the

strong nationalist sentiment to their support. One of their ways of doing so was to attempt to glorify China's past by interpreting it in accordance with their patterns. Thus they played up the *Shih Ching* or *Classic of Poetry*, one of the *Five Classics* from the dawn of the nation's history. They produced a version of it in the *pai hua*, or written vernacular, making much of the fact that it contained poems which voiced the aspirations and emotions of the common people. They stressed Po Chü-i, of the T'ang Dynasty, as a poet of the people. They re-read and re-wrote China's history in terms of the class struggle. They revived the popularity of one of the most widely read of Chinese novels, *Shui Hu Chuan*, attributed to the Yüan (Mongol) Dynasty, which glorified the deeds of refugees who rebelled against the corruption and evil social conditions of the decadent years of the Sung Dynasty. They lauded the T'ai P'ing movement as an upheaval of the oppressed. They brought new vigour to the Chinese language. It must be said, moreover, that the compulsory redistribution of land, taking it from landlords and dividing it among the peasants who cultivated it, was not without precedent in China's past.

Education in Communist ideology was undertaken on a gigantic scale. Much of it was in groups, in which there was public confession of past errors and of deviation from what, according to Communism, was correct thinking and action. Self-criticism and criticism by others were encouraged and even demanded. 'Brain-washing' of the more resistant was carried through, some of it in prison, some in locations akin to concentration camps, and some in schools for re-education. Public meetings were held again and again in local communities at which lectures on Communist topics were given, followed by discussion groups in which all were required to participate to make certain that the ideology was understood and accepted. Those accused of exploiting their neighbours were dealt with drastically, often in trials in which the populace was stimulated to ask for their execution. Many were required to pay wages which former employees alleged to have been withheld. Hundreds of thousands were executed as 'reactionaries' or oppressors of the people. Accusation was usually adjudged evidence of guilt and the burden of proof rested on the defendant to prove his innocence. Instruction in Communist ideology was made compulsory in the schools. Much of the education was by lengthy lectures and the reiteration, seemingly endless, of Communist convictions. Various organizations, such as those of youth and women, regimented special elements of the population into Communist patterns. 'Land reform' was carried through. By it the holdings of landlords were distributed among the peasant cultivators. Many of the landlords were killed for alleged oppression of former tenants and debtors.

Drastic changes were made in the economic structure. The formation of co-operatives among farmers was inaugurated and accelerated. Collective farms somewhat after the Russian pattern were created, at the outset chiefly in Manchuria. Increasing restrictions were placed on private business, and state enterprises were pushed. While in theory private capital and the bourgeoisie were permitted, they were allowed only under the leadership of the Communist Party and the proletariat and under state direction. More and more state enterprises – industrial, commercial, and financial – were created. In 1952 a ferocious attack directed chiefly against the bourgeoisie under the guise of a 'five-anti' campaign had as its announced purpose the elimination of bribery, tax evasion, fraud, theft of state assets, and leakage of state economic secrets. The bourgeoisie were accused of having sought to corrupt labour unions, to infiltrate units of the Party, and to demoralize Party members with luxuries and dissipation. The campaign was marked by huge mass meetings, public trials, and confessions. Through heavy fines and confiscations merchants and industrialists were stripped of most of their wealth. China's middle class was dying.

Since in the rapid expansion of the territory controlled by the People's Republic of China the membership of the Communist Party had also multiplied, there was grave danger that the corruption which was traditional in Chinese politics and government would creep into its ranks. This was heightened by the fact that many entered the Party from purely prudential reasons and that power led to the easing of the austerity which in the Yenan days had characterized the leadership and the rank and file. In 1952, accordingly, a purge of the government and the Party was carried through as an 'anti-corruption, anti-waste, and anti-bureaucratism struggle'.

In December 1949 a partial reorganization of the political divisions of China proper and Manchuria was made. Six major regions were created. Manchuria was North-East China. In what we have called China proper there were North China, North-West China, South-Central China, and South-West China. In addition there were the inner Mongolian Autonomous Region, directly subject to the Central People's Government in Peking, and Tibet. In October 1950 Tibet was invaded by a Communist army and in May 1951, the 'liberation' of that vast country having been deemed accomplished, a Chinese-Tibetan agreement was signed by which Tibet's autonomy was to be respected, religious freedom guaranteed, and the existing habits and customs were to be maintained, but by which China was to control Tibet's foreign relations and Tibetan military forces were to be integrated with those of China and to be under Chinese direction.

Communists were also attempting to win Chinese outside the country. Chinese were at the heart of the Communist guerilla movement in Malaya. Perhaps more important, Chinese youth were coming from South-East Asia and Indonesia to study in China. Presumably they would return to their homes as Communist missionaries.

By the middle of 1953 certain positive accomplishments could be chalked up to the credit of the Communist regime. Except for Formosa, territorial unity had been achieved and for the first time since the fall of the Manchus Peking's orders were being obeyed throughout the country. Railways, disorganized by long years of war, had been repaired and some new ones had been constructed. Major projects were under way in the north-west, in Shensi, Kansu, and Sinkiang. Progress had been made in the control of floods, especially those of the Yellow River, and much more ambitious plans were being put forward for reclamation, irrigation, and flood prevention. Much of this, to be sure, was by huge contingents of forced labour, among them thousands of intellectuals suspected of adherence to the old order. But at least it was being achieved. Inflation had been kept within bounds, prices stabilized, and devices adopted for insuring that the purchasing power of bank savings would be conserved. Taxes, while heavy, were being collected regularly and without the favouritism that had been rampant during earlier regimes. By 1953 there had been no extensive famine since the Communist 'liberation'. Yet the cities were being fed at the expense of the rural districts and food was being shipped to Russia. Gangsterism was being controlled and houses of prostitution eliminated. The army was well disciplined and its personnel was largely engaged in constructive public works. Education was being rapidly extended. Emphasis was placed upon technical schools. To increase literacy a method of mass education developed in the army was being applied to civilians. Athletic sports were fostered. Widespread efforts were being put forth to cope with disease and to improve public health and sanitation. Cities were cleaner than ever before. In urban areas public utilities were improved.

Yet this record had been made possible at a terrific cost in lives, liberty, moral integrity, and China's inherited traditions. At a conservative estimate from 3,000,000 to 5,000,000 had been executed in the first two years of Communist mastery. Most of this was by shootings in large groups which the public were encouraged or required to attend. In despair untold thousands had committed suicide. Many suffered from mental breakdowns. Class consciousness was created and nurtured and with it class hatred. Mass hysteria was fomented. A strict censorship of the printed page and the radio was enforced. In three respects something of the old China persisted: major attention was being given to winning the intelligentsia, including the students, and thus the tradition of rule by the educated was being maintained; the dream of creating a model human society which had been that of China's idealists from as far back as the Chou Dynasty and which was for the benefit of the people was still cherished; and much attention was paid to improving the lot of the common man, including the peasants. However, this was being done in ways which were more stringent than even those of China's earlier totalitarian advocates, the Legalists, and quite contrary to the relative *laissez-faire* of orthodox Confucianism, with its emphasis upon the family, its distrust of extremes, and its belief in the native goodness of men and the power of example and reason as contrasted with the appeal to physical force. Moreover, telling the truth was subordinated to the cause of the revolution. Lies were used boldly whenever they were deemed to serve the people's cause.

That there was dissatisfaction with the Communist regime was clear. By 1953 many who had welcomed it were disillusioned. Numbers of the educated were restless, for they found themselves regimented, compelled to work at tasks assigned them by the state, and with little prospect of following their own predilections. Thousands had taken refuge in Hongkong, where, with the defeat of Japan, British rule had been restored. Hundreds of thousands of peasants, finding that the heavy taxation was annulling, and perhaps more than annulling, whatever gains had come through the distribution of land and resenting the compulsory participation in co-operatives and collective farms, were engaging in the passive resistance in which the Chinese had long been adept. The National Government held out in Formosa and by 1953 was registering marked improvement in its administration of that island.

Yet, in the Anglo-Saxon meaning of that term, the Formosan government was not fully democratic. The Kuomintang still kept the main outlines of the structure which had been given it on Russian advice in the 1920's and which was modelled in part on that of the Russian Communist Party. Chiang Kai-shek's son, Chiang Ching-kuo, who had spent several years in Russia, was coming to the fore. He was bitterly anti-Communist, but he was believed to have autocratic tendencies. However, much more than the Chinese Communist Party, the National Government was a mixture, combining ideological elements from China's past, the U.S.S.R., and the democratic West, with the last by no means the least.

In 1953 there seemed to be no prospect of the disintegration or overthrow of the Communist regime. It was firmly sustained by a closely integrated and nation-wide party, by an army said to number 4,000,000, by a militia of approximately 14,000,000, by 'people's courts' and 'citizens' security committees', by about 3,000,000 propaganda workers, by a bureaucracy of from 20,000,000 to 30,000,000, and by a secret service – all features of the 'People's Democratic Dictatorship' and under the effective control of the leaders in Peking, of whom Mao Tse-tung was the chief. Factory labourers were organized and favoured, often at the expense of the countryside. Their economic condition was strikingly above what it had been before the Communists came to power. There was no prospect that Chiang Kai-shek and his Nationalists in Formosa would be strong enough to displace the Communists. His army was too small and the memories of Kuomintang rule were still too recent and too unhappy to permit any reasonable possibility that the Nationalists could retake the mainland.

By mid-1953 the People's Republic of China was looming large in the international scene. In general it was assertive in its dealings with governments outside the Russian bloc. It was vehemently determined not to be the prey of imperialist powers as China had been in the latter part of the nineteenth and the fore part of the twentieth century. In 1950 several powers in Europe and Asia clearly outside the Soviet sphere formally recognized it. Chief among these were Great

Britain and India. However, relations with neither of these were entirely amicable. Communist China found British Hongkong valuable as a door to the Western world, but it posed as the protector of the Chinese in British territories, especially in the Malayan Union and Singapore. India was disturbed by the occupation of Tibet by the Chinese Communists, for that might menace its northern frontiers. The French, too, were unhappy over the sympathy of the People's Republic of China for the Viet Minh campaign, led by Ho Chi Minh, which was engaging them in a major war to preserve some remnants of their rule in Indochina. Indeed, it was strongly suspected that as much tangible aid as sympathy was being given by the Chinese Communists to the Viet Minh.

However, by no means all governments had given recognition to the Chinese People's Republic. For example, in January 1950 the United States withdrew its consular and diplomatic staff from the mainland. It did this in part in protest against the arrest in Mukden of its consul and some of his staff and the expropriation of part of its property in Peking.

The major issues over which the People's Republic of China became embroiled with the rest of the world were connected with Korea. In the course of the final stages of their war against Japan the U.S.S.R. and the United States moved troops into Korea, for, as we have seen, that unhappy land had been part of the Japanese Empire since 1905, first as a protectorate and then, after 1910, by full annexation. For the purpose of disarming and repatriating the Japanese, Russian troops were moved into the north and American forces into the south, with the thirty-eighth parallel as the dividing line. That line, ostensibly intended to be temporary, was tragically enduring. A British-Russian-American conference in Moscow in December 1945 planned for a trusteeship of five years under Great Britain, Russia, China, and the United States, during which a democratic Korean government would be set up. A Soviet-American commission appointed to implement this programme could not reach an agreement. Communists trained by Russians set up the North Korea People's Government. In the south a government arose under American auspices. In November 1947, prodded by the United States and against Russian protests, the Assembly of the United Nations sent a commission to Korea with the purpose of forming a government for the entire country. North Korea refused to co-operate, but the commission engineered elections to a constituent assembly, the assembly adopted a constitution, and a regime was inaugurated with Syngman Rhee as President. In December 1948 this regime was recognized by the General Assembly of the United Nations as the only legitimate one in Korea. In September of that year the Democratic People's Republic was organized by the Communists in the north and claimed jurisdiction over the entire country. Russia, Poland, and Mongolia promptly recognized it. Both Russia and the United States withdrew their troops. Since there were now two governments, each aspiring to unite all Korea, the situation was decidedly unstable, and there was sporadic shooting along the thirty-eighth parallel.

In July 1950 fighting broke out which soon engaged much of the world and in which Communist China had a major role. Claiming that the South Koreans had attacked them, North Korean forces, equipped with Russian arms, poured across the border. Here was a crucial test for the United Nations. On 25 June, the day following the invasion, the Security Council of that organization met. The Russian representative had been boycotting the Council, and in his absence that body ordered the North Koreans to retire to their side of the thirty-eighth parallel. The United States, because of its predominant share in the Allied occupation of Japan, was the only power having a force near at hand to throw promptly into the breach. This it did, with General MacArthur in command. On the day in which he ordered American troops sent to Korea, President Truman commanded the American fleet 'to prevent any attack on Formosa', called on the National Government 'to cease all air and sea operations against the mainland', said that 'the

Seventh Fleet will see that this is done', declared that 'the determination of the future status of Formosa must await the restoration of security in the Pacific, a peace settlement with Japan, or consideration by the United Nations,' and ordered aid to the Philippines, France, 'and the associated states in Indochina' against the Communists. The United Nations asked its members to send contingents to Korea, and this several of them, including Great Britain, soon did. In the first few weeks the forces of the United Nations, ill-prepared, were pushed back almost to the southern tip of the peninsula. Then, in September, since reinforcements had arrived, by a dramatic landing at the port of Seoul that capital was retaken, and the United Nations army pushed north to the Yalu River, the boundary between Korea and China.

At that point, late in October and early in November 1950, the Chinese Communists stepped in. They chose to disregard the part which the United Nations was playing, claimed that the United States was the aggressor, and that the Americans were about to invade China through Manchuria. With troops whom they asserted were 'volunteers' they aided the North Koreans in driving back the armies of the United Nations. After several months a front was established not far from the thirty-eighth parallel. In this the Communists seem to have been moved in part by fear that the United Nations would invade China through Manchuria and seek to overthrow the People's Republic. By the methods of propaganda of which they were masters, the Chinese Communists sought to whip up popular emotions to 'resist America, aid Korea'. They stimulated subscriptions for equipment and planes to support the 'volunteers'. Exuberant over the fact that they had pushed back the armies of the United Nations – the first time that Chinese had ever been thus successful against Western forces – they declared the Americans to be a 'paper tiger' and in their news reports to the nation portrayed overwhelming victories. They and the Russians loudly accused the United States of using germ warfare in Manchuria, but refused the American proposal that a neutral commission of experts be appointed by the

United Nations to examine the evidence. They also charged Americans with gross atrocities and with bombing Manchuria.

Help from the United States to the National Government on Formosa was augmented. It took the form of financial assistance in a variety of ways, including economic reconstruction, and of arms and American advisers to the armed forces. Early in 1953, soon after his inauguration, President Eisenhower withdrew the curtain of the American fleet between Formosa and the China coast and his predecessor's restraint on the Nationalists from action against the mainland. It was still clear, however, that the Nationalists could not soon, if ever, unseat the Communists.

In the meantime diplomacy had not been inactive. In the United Nations the U.S.S.R. pressed the cause of the People's Republic of China and urged that the latter be substituted for the National Government in that body. It declared illegal the military action of the United Nations in Korea. It demanded that the North Koreans be seated in the Security Council of the United Nations in the discussions of terms of peace. This the United States effectively blocked, saying that the North Koreans must obey the Council and withdraw their troops as a prerequisite to such discussions. Washington consented to the sending by the People's Republic of China of representatives to the United Nations to bring to that body its complaints against the United States. However, it charged the People's Republic with being an aggressor in Korea and was adamant that this be decided before Peking's accusation be heard. The Chinese Communist delegates withdrew and on 1 February 1951, at the instance of the United States, the General Assembly of the United Nations declared that the People's Republic of China was an aggressor. That step was followed in May 1951, again at American insistence, by a recommendation of the General Assembly that all members of the United Nations abstain from sending to Communist China and North Korea arms or materials that could be used in the war.

On the eve of the first anniversary of the outbreak of the war in Korea a hint came from Russia that the Communists might welcome negotiations looking towards an armistice. Before many weeks these were begun. They dragged on into 1952. Accord was achieved on some points, but an impasse was reached over the return of prisoners of war. The United States insisted that no prisoner should be returned against his will. Many North Koreans and Chinese held by the United Nations' forces, so it was said, loathed Communism, and it was declared that to insist upon their repatriation would mean for them almost certain death. India, which had long been seeking to mediate, proposed that such prisoners be turned over to a neutral nation, and this found favour in the United Nations with all but the Communist bloc. To it the People's Republic of China, the U.S.S.R., and the latter's satellites would not consent and negotiations broke down. However, in April 1953, an exchange of some of the sick and wounded prisoners was effected and negotiations for an armistice were resumed. If such an armistice were achieved it would be only military, and negotiations for a political settlement would need to follow and would probably not quickly be completed.

And here we must leave our story. It is tantalizing to have to stop *in medias res*. Yet the historian can only record what has happened. If he endeavours to peer into the future he has abandoned for the moment the role of historian and has essayed that of the prophet. The first half of the year 1953 was not one of major transition. We pause there because that is the time when these pages were written.

EPILOGUE

THE restrictions imposed by the fact of living within time have compelled us to end our narrative with a semi-colon. Yet there may be some advantage in looking back over the course thus far traversed and seeking to view it from the perspective won through the rapid survey of this little volume.

As background for the cultural and political revolution which has been our primary theme, we first attempted a summary of the development of the Chinese and their civilization before the disturbing impact of the Occident. We saw its beginnings in a past only dimly discerned. We watched it take shape under the moulding force of great thinkers and administrators. We noted that shortly before the time of Christ what we call the Chinese Empire had brought within its fold most of what we have called China proper and on more than one front had passed beyond it. We remarked on the dream of China's great, a dream passed on by them to the multitude, that all mankind should be brought within one inclusive realm controlled by one civilization, a civilization which was the norm for mankind. Shut off by geography from intimate contact with other peoples of high civilizations which had not been borrowed from them, the Chinese quite understandably viewed their culture as that norm. Many contributions came from the outside, notably from India, the nearest large neighbour, in the form of Buddhism and the ethical, thought, and art patterns associated with it. Yet in the main the culture of China was indigenous.

By the middle of the tenth century of the Christian era that culture presented the features which, with relatively slight modifications, it was to retain until the close of the nineteenth century. It was shaped primarily by Confucianism. Confucianism was supported and continued by a governmental structure which in theory and to a large degree in practice was committed to it. That government was closely integrated with an educational system, also controlled by Confucianism, through which, by highly competitive examinations, the bureaucracy was recruited which administered the Empire.

Then came the impact of the aggressive West. This first made itself felt vaguely in the thirteenth century and more markedly in the sixteenth century. But it was not until the middle of the nineteenth century that the Occident began so to impose itself on China that the culture of that empire showed signs of strain. By the twentieth century the revolution was commencing which in the next five decades moved on at an ever-accelerated pace. Early in the century two of the chief props of Confucianism were removed, the Confucian political structure and the Confucian educational system. In that age when the impact of the West was working revolution in almost every people on the face of the globe, the culture of China was disintegrating more rapidly and extensively than was that of any other major civilized folk. This seems to have been due in large degree to the nature of Confucianism and of the society which it had created. As a result a near approach to a cultural vacuum was created.

Into the vacuum first came the culture of the West either directly or, somewhat distorted, through Japan. It was brought partly by merchants, partly by diplomats, partly by Christian missionaries, and partly by students returning from the West or from Japan. For a time it looked as though the Chinese would create a culture in which features from their own past would be combined with Western democracy, science, and Christianity. That was the prospect at the beginning of the fourth decade of the century.

The incipient culture was weakened, perhaps fatally, by the determination of Japan to be dominant in the East of Asia. A fresh near-vacuum was created. Into it moved Communism, an ideology which had originated in the West and which had mastered Russia when in World War I in that empire a power vacuum had been created, also by the impact of the West. Communism came to China by way of Russia and by 1950 was in full control except in Formosa, where a remnant of the previous attempt at adjustment to the West held out, aided by the chief champion of the Occident, the United States. In 1953 Communism was firmly in control and was closely allied with Russia. It was bringing the most drastic re-shaping of the Chinese which that people had ever experienced.

What the future held in store no one could certainly know. It might be that the Communist conquest portended a similar fate for Japan, South-East Asia, and the fringing islands. That is what the Communists hoped and what they predicted would happen not only in Asia but also in the rest of the world. Yet many observers did not share their confidence. They hoped and believed that Communism would be checked and that ultimately the Chinese would throw off the Communist yoke with its Russian tie and would move once more in the direction from which the Japanese attack had diverted them, towards a fruitful combination of their own past with dynamic elements from the democratic West and from Christianity.

BIBLIOGRAPHY

FROM the enormous bibliography in Western languages on China we must endeavour to select a few books, all of them in English, which can serve as a guide for those who may wish to pursue further some of the subjects to which these chapters have been an introduction.

For a general survey, containing extensive bibliographies, see K. S. Latourette, *The Chinese: Their History and Culture* (London, Macmillan & Co., 2 vols, 1934. The third, revised edition was published in New York by The Macmillan Co. in 1946).

Extremely useful for reference is S. Couling, *The Encyclopaedia Sinica* (London, Oxford University Press, 1917).

For the pre nineteenth century China an admirable survey is C. P. Fitzgerald, *China. A Short Cultural History* (London, The Cresset Press, 1935).

On the Chinese classical books of the Chou Dynasty older translations into English, still standard, are by James Legge, *The Chinese Classics* (first edition, 5 vols., Hongkong, 1861–72; second edition, revised, 5 vols., Oxford, London, 1893, 1895; also vols 3, 16, 27, 28 of *The Sacred Books of the East*, Oxford, 1879, 1882, 1885). More recent are Arthur Waley, *The Analects of Confucius, Translated and annotated* (London, George Allen & Unwin, 1938), and Arthur Waley, *Three Ways of Thought in Ancient China* (London, George Allen & Unwin, 1939).

Indispensable for the Ch'ing Dynasty is A. W. Hummel (editor), *Eminent Chinese of the Ch'ing Dynasty* (2 vols, Washington, D.C., United States Government Printing Office, 1943, 1944).

On the impact of the West on China a standard comprehensive coverage from 1834 to 1911, also giving much of China's domestic history, is H. B. Morse, *The International Relations of the Chinese Empire* (3 vols., London, Longmans, Green & Co., 1910, 1913, 1918). Important is S. F. Wright,

Bibliography

Hart and the Chinese Customs (Belfast, William Mullan & Son, 1950). Standard for Christian missions from the seventh century to 1928 is K. S. Latourette, *A History of Christian Missions in China* (London, Society for Promoting Christian Knowledge, 1929). Treaties and related documents are in J. V. A. MacMurray, *Treaties and Agreements with and concerning China*, 1894–1919 (2 vols, Oxford University Press, American Branch, 1921), and a continuation of the latter, compiled by the Carnegie Endowment for International Peace, *Treaties and Agreements with and concerning China*, 1919–29. See also P. Joseph, *Foreign Diplomacy in China*, 1894–1900 (London, George Allen & Unwin, 1928).

On the revolution of 1911–12 an interesting contemporary account is P. H. Kent, *The Passing of the Manchus* (London, Edward Arnold, 1912).

For Sun Yat-sen, see his *San Min Chu I*, *The Three Principles of the People*, translated by F. W. Price (Shanghai, China Committee, Institute of Pacific Relations, 1927), and the best life in English, Lyon Sharman, *Sun Yat-sen, His Life and Meaning, a Critical Biography* (New York, the John Day Co. 1934).

On the events of the mid-1920's, see the contemporary H. O. Chapman, *The Chinese Revolution*, 1926–27. *A Record of the Period under Communist Control as seen from the Nationalist Capital, Hankow* (London, Constable & Co., 1928), and an important later study, B. I. Schwartz, *Chinese Communism and the Rise of Mao* (Harvard University Press, 1951).

For Chiang Kai-shek, see a sympathetic biography, S. I. Hsiung, *The Life of Chiang Kai-shek* (London, Peter Davies, 1948), and Chiang Kai-shek, *China's Destiny and Chinese Economic Theory*, translated by two Chinese with notes and commentary by P. Jaffe (New York, Roy Publishers, 1947). Jaffe is very unsympathetic to Chiang Kai-shek.

For one stage of the Japanese invasion of China, see H. S. Quigley, *Far Eastern War*, 1937–1941 (Boston, World Peace Foundation, 1942).

For developments in Manchuria, see F. C. Jones, *Manchuria since 1931* (Oxford University Press, 1949).

Bibliography

For an official account and selected documents, see the 'White Paper', *United States Relations With China With Special Reference to the Period* 1944–1949, *Based on the Files of the Department of State* (Washington, Department of State Publication 3573, Far Eastern Series 30, August, 1949).

Among the flood of books on Communism in China the following are among the more useful: E. Snow, *Red Star Over China* (New York, Random House, 1938), a first-hand sympathetic report; E. Hunter, *Brain-Washing in Red China: the Calculated Destruction of Men's Minds* (New York, the Vanguard Press, 1951), also first-hand, but highly critical; O. B. Van der Sprenkel, R. Guillain, M. Lindsay, *New China: Three Views* (New York, John Day Co., 1951, the American edition of a British book), by first-hand, somewhat sympathetic observers; and C. Brandt, B. Schwartz, and J. K. Fairbank, *A Documentary History of Chinese Communism* (London, George Allen & Unwin, 1952).

INDEX

Afghanistan, 38
Africa, 12, 13, 54, 88, 151
Alaska, 176, 179
Aleutians, 176, 179
Americas, the, 12, 13, 46, 54, 79
Amoy, 63, 151, 181
Amur river, 67, 88
Anhui, 159
Annam, 19, 43, 80
Annamese, 57
Arab states, 118
Asia, 12, 17, 20, 34, 37, 38, 42, 54, 55, 57, 89, 97, 108, 151, 223
Australasia, 13
Australia, 12, 108, 177, 178
Austria, 125, 129, 130, 132, 133

Balkans, 97
Bangkok, 60
Bannerman, 115
Belgium, 134, 174
Belgians, 89
Boer war, 97
Bokhara, 38
Bonin Islands, 82
Borodin, 140, 145, 146
Boxer rebellion, and aftermath, 93, 94, 95, 97, 99, 100, 101, 107, 109, 110, 130, 133, 151, 152
Brahmaputra river, 21
British, the, 43, 76, 77, 81, 82, 83, 91, 104, 110, 136, 137, 145, 151, 162–3, 174, 178, 214; see also Great Britain.

British Commonwealth, 178
British Empire, 61, 134, 177
British Isles, 78, 107, 110, 150
Buddhism, 10, 30, 36, 37, 39, 40, 41, 42, 48, 55, 57, 73, 102, 118, 138, 155, 209, 221
Burlingame, Anson, 77
Burma, 17, 19, 43, 80, 81, 118, 173, 174, 176, 178, 179, 182

Cairo, 181
California, 80
Cambaluc, 41
Cambodia, 80
Canton, 18, 45, 60, 61, 62, 63, 64, 68, 89, 91, 92, 107, 113, 130, 131, 132, 136, 140, 142, 144, 148, 170, 181, 182, 203
Ceylon, 42, 78, 118, 173, 178
Ch'ang-an, 38, 39, 94
Chang Chih-tung, 91, 101
Chang Hsüeh-liang, 148, 153, 160, 161, 165, 166, 182, 196
Chang Hsün, 129
Chang Kuo-t'ao, 186
Chang Tso-lin, 131, 134, 139, 147, 148, 153, 160, 196
Changsha, 143, 145, 187
Chekiang, 142
Ch'ên Tu-hsiu, 142, 143, 144, 146, 147, 157
Cheng-feng movement, 186
Chengtu, 112
Chiang Ching-kuo, 215

227

*The following pages
describe other Pelicans which
should interest readers
of this book*

UR OF THE CHALDEES

A 27

An account of the excavations that have taken place in Ur over a number of years, and particularly the recent expeditions sponsored by the University Museum of Pennsylvania and the British Museum under the directorship of the author of this book.   (2s)

'Reading *Ur of the Chaldees* one is filled with awe at the richness and perfection of man's workmanship 5,000 years ago; at the immensity of man's knowledge to-day in piecing together the scattered remains of the past.' – *Time and Tide*

DIGGING UP THE PAST

A 4

In this book Sir Leonard Woolley explains in detail what archaeology is all about, describing the preliminary organization of a 'dig,' the delicate processes of getting inside a site, and the subsequent analysis of the evidence which has been brought to light. The text is illustrated by a fine series of plates covering many of the processes, and the discoveries of archaeology in Ur, Italy, Palestine, Knossos, Egypt, and Scandinavia.   (2s)

A FORGOTTEN KINGDOM

A 261

An important new book by Sir Leonard Woolley which was published for the first time as a Pelican in 1953. It is a record of the results obtained from the excavation of two mounds, Atchana, and Al Mina, in the Turkish Hatay, with 24 plates and numerous text figures.   (2s 6d)

THE PREHISTORY OF EAST AFRICA

Sonia Cole

A 316

Probably more is known about the very earliest phases of man's existence in East Africa than in any other part of the world. The geological background, including evidence of past climates, provides a framework for the dating of man's skeletal remains and material cultures. From the time of the first pebble-industries, nearly a million years ago, the progress of human skill is here traced until stone tools were gradually replaced by iron, perhaps no more than a thousand years ago. This is the first book to treat the prehistory of East Africa as a whole. (2s 6d)

ISLAM

Alfred Guillaume

A 311

In this book Professor Guillaume provides the essentials for an understanding of the Arab peoples. He deals in turn with Mohammed, the founder of Islam; the Quran, its holy book; the evolution of Mohammedanism as a system of faith, law, religion and philosophy; the varying schools of thought and the intense devotional life that have grown up within it; and discusses the changes which are now taking place in the Islamic viewpoint as the Muslim peoples prepare to take their full part in the modern world. (2s)

THE ANCIENT WORLD

T. R. Glover

A 120

The civilization of the Western World was born many centuries ago on the shores of the Mediterranean, and in this survey of its origin Dr Glover has reconstructed the achievements and discoveries of the Greeks and Romans. He was a scholar of great distinction who knew his sources intimately, but he reinforces his book-knowledge of the Ancient World by many prolonged journeys in those historic regions. What he has to tell us, therefore, of the growth and influence of these empires of antiquity is illuminated by his own vivid response to the environment where so much history was made. This genius for bringing the past to life is the quality, above all others, which made Dr Glover so vivid an historian, and this genius was never more brilliantly revealed than in *The Ancient World*.*   (2s 6d)

THE ARCHAEOLOGY OF PALESTINE

W. F. Albright

A 199

The tiny country on the Eastern Mediterranean coast which has played so outstanding a part in human history has yielded up in recent years so many of the secrets of its past that a popular summary of the results has long been overdue. Professor Albright, who has himself done so much to bring the treasures of its past to light, here tells the story of their gradual unearthing, of the building up of a connected picture of Palestine's history, and of the light thus thrown on human history in general and on the Old Testament story. An introductory chapter of the greatest interest tells how the archaeologist sets about his task.   (2s 6d)

* NOT FOR SALE IN THE U.S.A.

While each volume is complete in itself, the whole series has
been planned to provide an intelligent and consecutive guide
to the development of English society in all its aspects. The
eight volumes are:

1. ROMAN BRITAIN *by Professor Ian Richmond*, King's College, Newcastle-on-Tyne

2. THE BEGINNINGS OF ENGLISH SOCIETY (from the
   Anglo-Saxon Invasion) *by Dorothy Whitelock*, Fellow of St
   Hilda's College, Oxford

3. ENGLISH SOCIETY IN THE EARLY MIDDLE AGES *by Doris
   Mary Stenton*, Lecturer at Reading University

4. ENGLAND IN THE LATE MIDDLE AGES *by A. R. Myers*,
   Lecturer at Liverpool University

5. TUDOR ENGLAND *by S. T. Bindoff*, Professor of History at
   Queen Mary College, London

6. ENGLAND IN THE SEVENTEENTH CENTURY *by Maurice
   Ashley, M.A.*

7. ENGLAND IN THE EIGHTEENTH CENTURY *by J. H.
   Plumb*, Fellow of Christ's College, Cambridge

8. ENGLAND IN THE NINETEENTH CENTURY *by David
   Thomson*, Fellow of Sidney Sussex College, Cambridge

*'As a portent in the broadening of popular culture the influence of this
wonderful series has yet to receive full recognition and precise asses-
ment. No venture could be more enterprising or show more confidence in
the public's willingness to purchase thoughtful books. ...'* The
Listener

The price of the volumes varies from 2s to 2s 6d
Some are obtainable in a bound edition at 7s 6d each